PROVEN!
God is Real
&
Jesus is God

*New evidence from science,
history & philosophy*

Michelle Joseph

Copyright, Legal Notice and Disclaimer:

PROVEN! God is Real and Jesus is God.
Copyright © 2015 by Michelle Joseph.

All rights reserved. No part of this book may be reproduced in any form by any electronic or mechanical means (including photocopying, recording, or information storage and retrieval) without permission in writing from the author.

While all attempts have been made to verify the information provided in this publication, the author and publisher assume no responsibility for errors or omissions.

Contents

Copyright, Legal Notice and Disclaimer: ii
Preface & Dedication vii
Introduction 1
PART 1: DOES GOD EXIST? 5
Chapter 1: Investigating Truth 7
   How do we investigate whether God exists? 7
   What do we mean by 'God'? 9
   Does it matter what we believe? 10
   Is there such a thing as religious truth? 12
   Can there be just one true religion? 13
   Religion is a product of social and cultural conditioning 15
   Bible references 15
Chapter 2: Scientific Evidence for God 17
   Where did we come from? Examining the cosmos… 17
   The Big Bang = A Big Banger? 17
   Did the universe create itself? 18
   Created by God? 19
   God causing things to exist now? 20
   If something exists, then God exists 21
   Do science and the Bible conflict? 22
   Conditions for life 23
   Intelligent and complex design 26
   Conclusion 29
Chapter 3: Humanistic Evidence for God 31
   Morality 31
      Morality a product of evolution? 33
      Is moral relativism an option? 33
      No such thing as human rights? 34

Love, beauty & desire for God	35
No logic without God	37
Life is pointless without God	38
Conclusion	39

PART 2: INVESTIGATING RELIGION & CHRISTIANITY 41

Chapter 4: How To Find Religious Truth 43
    False religions 43
    True religion 45
    Investigating Christianity 46

Chapter 5: The Bible & New Testament – True or False? 49
  Can we trust the New Testament gospels? 49
    Timing too early for gospels to be legends 50
    Honest accounts 52
    Detailed accounts 53
    Reliable eyewitnesses 54
    Rigorous tests for inclusion 54
  The disciples persecution 55
  Archaeological evidence 57
  Extra biblical writings 60
  Manuscript evidence 61
  Fulfilled prophecy 63
  The Bible's internal consistency 65
  Jesus' assurance 65
  The Bible's ability to transform lives 66
  Conclusion 67

Chapter 6: Evidence Jesus is God 69
  Fulfilled prophecy 69
  Miracles 71
  Proof of the resurrection 73

Contents

Chapter 7: Objections to the Bible 79
   You can't take the Bible literally 79
   Isn't the Bible full of contradictions? 80
   Has evolution disproved the Bible? 81
   The Bibles teachings are outdated 84
Chapter 8: Doubts & Objections to Christianity 85
   How could a good God allow suffering? 85
   Evil provides evidence for God? 88
   Aren't miracles impossible? 89
   Why doesn't God do miracles more often to prove His existence? 91
   How can a loving God send people to Hell? 92
   Religion is divisive 95
   I don't like Church and/or Christians 97
   Doesn't religion cause violence? 98
   Christianity is an emotional crutch 101
   Is religion a product of evolution? 102
   Becoming a Christian will restrict my freedom 104
   I'm not good enough to be a Christian 106
   Conclusion 107
PART 3: WHAT NOW? 111
Chapter 9: Accepting or Rejecting God 111
   Who is the Christian God? 111
   Why did God create us? 112
   Heaven & Hell 114
      What is Heaven like? 114
      The 'New Earth' 114
      Do good people go to Heaven? 115
      Is Hell real? 116
      Who goes to Hell? 117
      Is Satan real? 117
   Salvation, Sin & Jesus 118

- *What is sin?* 118
- *Are you a sinner?* 119
- *Repentance* 119
- *Accepting Jesus for salvation* 120
- *The sinner's prayer* 123
- *Know you are saved* 124
- *Doubts about Christianity* 125
- *Rejecting God* 126

A New Life 127
- *Christian Community & Church* 128
- *The Bible* 129
- *Prayer* 129
- *Promises of God* 130
- *Tell others* 133
- *Discovering your purpose* 134
- *Growing in Christ* 136
- *Trials & suffering* 137
- *Staying the distance* 139

Chapter 10: Parting thoughts 141
- Where else would we go? 141

Acknowledgements 143
About the Author 145

Preface & Dedication

I am not going to hide the fact that I'm a Christian and that ultimately I believe the evidence points to the truth of Christianity. However, because I have a viewpoint doesn't mean that what I am writing is untrue - the evidence should be evaluated on its own merit. All books have a viewpoint as the author is seeking to communicate an idea or story they care about or consider important.

I was a Christian prior to writing this book and the way I came to know Jesus was not through scientific evidence or logical reasoning but through the love of God. Having examined the objective scientific evidence however, I am now convinced more than ever that God exists. My faith has been strengthened and my spirit awakened in light of this knowledge. We are called to love God with our minds as well as our hearts and souls (Matt 22:37). As a result, the closeness I feel to God knowing with so much certainty He exists and the amazing evidence He has given us is hard to describe. It has also given me new confidence in sharing my faith with others, knowing that science and logic are on my side. The Bible tells us to 'always be prepared to make a defence to anyone who asks you for a reason for the hope that is in you' (1 Peter 3:15, English Standard Version). Therefore I pray if you are a Christian you will feel more equipped and as well as closer to God after reading this book.

If you are not a Christian, I pray you will be more open to God after reading this book and will continue your own search for Him.

> 'And you will know the truth, and the truth will set you free.'
> (John 8:32)

This book is dedicated to my beloved late grandfather Colin Rawlinson whose passing highlighted to me that time is short and that millions are dying without knowing Jesus.

Introduction

Is there a God? This is perhaps the most important question you will ever be faced with. How you answer this question will determine all parts of your life, how you choose to live during your time on earth and where you will spend eternity (if such a thing exists).

Related questions that often lead people to God include:

- How did I get here?
- Why am I here?
- What is my purpose?
- How should I live my life?
- What happens when I die?

That so many people go their whole lives without seriously considering these questions is astonishing, considering the answers impact all areas of your life such as:

- How you will live your life
- How you relate to yourself and others
- How you spend your time & resources
- Your worldview
- Your beliefs & attitude
- Where you will spend eternity

Perhaps the most important of these questions is the last one – 'where you will spend eternity'. If eternity or an 'afterlife' exists – it is going to be for a very long time! It is hard for our minds to grasp the concept of something being never ending or eternal. We could think of our lives like one grain of sand and the beach as eternity.

Before we start to consider these questions, I'd like to share with you 'Pascal's Wager'[1] formulated by the French Mathematician Blaise Pascal (this is commonly taught in 1st year philosophy class and likewise you may also have learnt about Pascal's triangle at school).

It goes like this… By virtue of existing, we must bet either way that 1) God exists or 2) God doesn't exist. Pascal assumes that we cannot know with 100% certainty if either position is true. If we bet 'God exists' and we get it right – we 'win' big i.e. we spend eternity in Heaven. If we get it wrong, we potentially lose small i.e. missing out on some earthly pleasures (personally I enjoy life way more with God than without Him but that's for you to decide…)

If we bet 'God doesn't exist' and we get it right, we win small i.e. we get to live how we want in this life and not worry about God. If we get it wrong – we lose really big – because we spend eternity in Hell. This can be expressed in a matrix as below:

	God exists	**God doesn't exist**
Get it right	Eternity in Heaven	Small win on earth
Get it wrong	Eternity in Hell	Small loss on earth

This is based on eternity being a VERY long time compared to the very short time we have on earth. Anything compared to infinity (eternity) is essentially zero. Whatever we could possibly gain or lose in this life will be worth NOTHING in comparison to eternity. Surely it makes more sense to base our decision on how it will impact eternity

---

1 http://en.wikipedia.org/wiki/Pascal's_Wager

Introduction

or 'after life' than to worry about this life? Pascal based his wager on the Christian God of the Bible.

While I'm not asking you to believe based on Pascal's theory – I am saying it is worth CONSIDERING whether there could be a God and whether the truth claims of Jesus and the Bible have any merit. In light of potential eternity in either Heaven or Hell, it would be worth at least looking into these things don't you think? You might still decide there is no God but at least you will have done 'due diligence' and can happily live your life with your decision.

I pray this book will prove useful to you. I encourage you to also do your own research and even pray and ask God (if you believe there could be a God) to reveal truth to you!

PART 1

DOES GOD EXIST?

CHAPTER 1

Investigating Truth

How do we investigate whether God exists?

Given that no one has ever seen God – He doesn't have a physical body - how would we begin to investigate whether or not He exists? We perceive the existence of most things through our natural senses such as sight, smell, taste or hearing, however God is not part of the natural world – therefore He can't be perceived that way. Does this mean He doesn't exist?

Not necessarily. Our senses don't give us the full picture about who 'we' are either. We can see our bodies but we are more than our bodies. Bodies change and we may even lose a limb but that doesn't mean we become less 'us'. We are not our brains either – some people get brain damage but they are still fully a person. We cannot isolate a single cell or group of cells and point to it as being 'us'– likewise God cannot be pinpointed in that way.

If someone could not see us or perceive us with their senses, how might they determine we existed?

Perhaps they might find things we have created such as a painting, a book or meal we have cooked as evidence of us. They might find people we know who testify to our existence. Perhaps they would check historical records or a birth registrar. They might observe our home and find traces that we exist (in my case, they may find a mess..!)

To determine if God exists, we also start with what we can see. We can observe ourselves, the world around us and history to see if there is any evidence or clues that point to the existence of God. We can use the objective tools of science and philosophy to assess this evidence and what it tells us about the likelihood of there being a God or not. As defined below, science deals with the physical and natural world whilst philosophy analyses claims using logic and rational reasoning.

Definition of Science:

> "The intellectual and practical activity encompassing the systematic study of the structure and behaviour of the physical and natural world through observation and experiment."[2]

Definition of Philosophy:

> "The rational investigation of the truths and principles of being, knowledge, or conduct."[3]

Some people claim that because science cannot prove conclusively either way whether God exists –God must not exist. However, by its own definition, science can only test and examine the natural and physical world we live in. As God is 'super' natural and lies outside of the natural realm, He cannot be examined through the material world in a laboratory. Despite this limitation, science CAN examine humanity and the natural world we live in to see whether we can find evidence for a Creator. We can look at the 'effects' of God, which we can observe with science such as the universe we live in.

The reason and logic employed by philosophy, are also useful tools to help us determine whether God exists as well as the truth claims of particular religions. For example, to be valid, the claims of any belief system must not logically contradict each other. For instance, the goal of Buddhism is to rid yourself of all desires and cravings[4]. However, in order to do this, you must have the DESIRE to rid yourself of all

---

[2] http://www.oxforddictionaries.com/definition/english/science
[3] http://dictionary.reference.com/browse/philosophy
[4] http://en.wikipedia.org/wiki/Buddhism#Criticism_and_apologetics

desires – this is illogical and contradictory.[5]

We can also look to historical and archaeological evidence to support truth claims. For example, the book of Mormon teaches that Jesus appeared in North America after his crucifixion and resurrection.[6] However, there is no archaeological evidence to support the book's claims of links to North America.[7]

Once we have gathered the evidence, we can then begin to make conclusions. How will we come to a conclusion to decide either for or against the existence of God? We will use 'proof beyond reasonable doubt' which is the highest standard of proof of most legal systems as required for criminal convictions. There can still be a slight doubt but only to the extent it would not affect a reasonable person's belief regarding the defendant's guilt.[8]

Very rarely is 100% certainty possible, however I believe we can know 'beyond reasonable doubt' whether God exists. After all, if God is real and He wants us to know Him, He will surely leave clues.

What do we mean by 'God'?

Oxford Dictionary definition:

1. (In Christianity and other monotheistic religions) the creator and ruler of the universe and source of all moral authority; the supreme being.

2. (god) (In certain other religions) a superhuman being or spirit worshipped as having power over nature or human fortunes; a deity: e.g. a moon god

---

5 http://www.gotquestions.org/correct-religion.html
6 http://www.mormon.org.au/faq/christ-in-america
7 http://en.wikipedia.org/wiki/Archaeology_and_the_Book_of_Mormon
8 http://en.wikipedia.org/wiki/Reasonable_doubt

Does it matter what we believe?

Wholeheartedly, yes! As a psychology graduate, I am well aware of the impact our beliefs have on our lives.

We all have a great many beliefs. Some may be correct, some may not be. Some may serve us, some may not. Whatever our beliefs are, we act on them. If I believe a red light means 'stop' when driving, I will stop. If I believe 'green' means go, I will go. Getting these beliefs wrong could lead to disastrous actions. I could harm myself and others. The same is true with spiritual beliefs. They can set the course of our lives and determine how we will live and what will happen when we die. Getting this wrong could also have disastrous consequences.

How we arrive at our beliefs varies. Some people adopt the beliefs of their culture, friends and families. They accept them as true because other people believe the same thing but don't give much thought to whether the beliefs are correct or not. Others arrive at beliefs based on past experiences and form conclusions based on these beliefs. These conclusions may be either correct or incorrect depending on how they were interpreted. For example, if abused as a child, they may conclude that all people can't be trusted and avoid forming close love relationships as an adult. It may take some effort to form new beliefs that allow them to trust people.

The same applies to beliefs about God. Perhaps you experienced 'fire and brimstone' preaching as a child or young adult and concluded that God is angry and judgemental. Or perhaps we have adopted the attitudes and lifestyles of our parents and society whom live as if there is no God. Maybe because we can't see God, we conclude He must not exist. Alternatively, we may have been brought up in a family that had strong Muslim, Buddhist or Christian beliefs and we have simply adopted these without giving a lot of thought as to whether they're true or not. It is a good idea to examine your beliefs around God and religion and how these might have been formed.

Investigating Truth

Some beliefs we hold, may have been formed through critical thought and reasoning. For example, although we can't see gravity, we can observe its effects. We can see that when we drop something it falls to the floor. We may have also read and understood the scientific theory behind gravity. We believe in gravity so if we want to live, we will avoid jumping from tall buildings! This book will use critical thought, reasoning and science to investigate questions concerning God, religion and the Bible. You can then form your own conclusions based on the evidence.

It is unfortunately true that some people, even when presented with substantial proof may still be unwilling to consider a different worldview for various reasons. They may not wish to have different beliefs to their family or friends, or may not like what adopting new beliefs mean for their lives. Consider how open you are to adopting new beliefs if you were presented with substantial evidence in favour of a different worldview.

I heard an amusing parable about a man who believed he was dead. His wife could not convince him he was alive so she took him to a medical doctor. The medical doctor examined him, told him he had a pulse, was in good physical health and was definitely alive but the man would not believe him. The wife then took him to a psychologist. The psychologist explained to the man that he could know for sure he was alive as dead people didn't bleed. To prove to him that dead people don't bleed, the psychologist took him to a morgue and pricked the skin of the dead people which didn't bleed. Upon seeing this, the man confirmed he believed dead people didn't bleed. The psychologist then pricked the skin of the man and he bled. The psychologist asked what he believed now – the man proclaimed - "well, I'll be… dead people do bleed after all!".

Examine yourself for a moment to see how open you are to questioning some long held beliefs you may have. If given 'proof beyond reasonable doubt', would you be willing to revise some of these beliefs?

Is there such a thing as religious truth?

Will it be possible to recognise the truth if we find it? Does such a thing even exist?

First we must establish that 'absolute truth' exists. If it does not, then we will not be able to identify truth if we find it.

Absolute truth is defined as an inflexible reality with fixed, unalterable facts. It is true for all people, at all times and in all places. It is true whether someone believes it is true or not and matches reality. For example, it is absolutely true there are no square circles or round squares. 2+2=4 for all people at all times, whether they believe it is true or not.

'Relative truth' in contrast, is truth that is true for only certain people at certain times and places. It may be true now but it may not have been true in the past and may not be true in the future – it is subject to change and according to the different perspectives which people have.

Relative truth is the category some people put religious truth into. They believe God or religion can be true for some people but not others. They may also believe that all religions are equally valid and true.

However, in reality, nothing can be 'relatively' true – it is either absolutely true or it is absolutely not true. The claim 'truth is relative' actually contradicts itself as it would need to be 'absolutely true' in order to be true. If we say 'truth is relative' then the statement itself is relative, meaning it's not true for all people all the time. A true statement will not contradict itself in this way. Truth is therefore shown to be 'absolute' rather than 'relative'. Opinions are 'relative' but truth is not.

If 'relative truth' is shown to be contradictory, then 'relative truth' statements about spiritual matters will also be contradictory. An example of a relative truth statement on spirituality is 'all religions lead to God' or 'all religions are equally true'.

In fact, it is impossible for all religions to be true as they contradict each other. Some religions teach there are many gods, others that there is just one. Others teach that God is in nature, others that you can become a god. Some religions teach Jesus is not God, Christianity teaches Jesus is God. There cannot be both, only one God and many Gods. Likewise, Jesus cannot be God and not God at the same time. Jesus claims that He alone is the Way, the Truth and the Life (John 14:6). He cannot be right about this as well as all other religions being right that He is not God.

Therefore some religions must be true and others false. Religions also teach different things about Heaven, Hell, reincarnation, life after death, what God is like, how the world was created etc. They cannot all be right if they contradict each other. This is not to say that many religions don't have elements of truth in them – as many of them surely do. Whilst many religions claim to be the 'true religion', this doesn't make them so. They must be able to back up the claim with evidence which is what we'll be investigating in this book.

Can there be just one true religion?

Some people object to a particular religion because it claims to have the 'truth' and that 'no one religion can know the truth'. They often believe that those who say their religion is correct and others are wrong are narrow-minded and intolerant. They may hold that people shouldn't try to convert others to their religions and that they should instead be accepting of all religions as 'no one religion is superior to others'.

At the heart of these claims is religious pluralism – the belief that all religious worldviews are equally valid.[9] Pluralists usually believe there are multiple paths to God.

---

9 http://en.wikipedia.org/wiki/Religious_pluralism

However do we really believe that religions requiring child sacrifice or torture are not inferior to any other religion (including atheism)? Most people would say religions requiring child sacrifice or torture are evil and should be stopped.

Not only is pluralism unreasonable - like claims about relative truth - pluralist claims are also self-defeating and contradictory. Whilst pluralism can seem 'tolerant' on the surface, religious pluralism itself is another form of truth claim. Religious pluralists are claiming that THEIR version of the truth is correct and that others who don't believe in pluralism are wrong. Hence they are doing the very thing (holding an exclusive viewpoint) they are trying to stop.

Similar reasoning can be applied to claims like 'no belief can be universally true for everyone'. This is again self-defeating because the question becomes – is the belief 'no belief can be universally true for everyone' – true for everyone? It is a contradiction to try to impose such a belief on everyone if 'no belief can be universally true'. In addition, how does the person making this claim KNOW that 'no belief can be universally true for everyone' unless they're in the place of God..?

Similarly, if holding the view that one's own religious beliefs are correct and others are wrong is 'narrow minded', then holding the view that 'no single religion holds the truth' is also narrow minded as both camps think they are right and that others should believe as they do.

Therefore all claims about religious pluralism are illogical and contradictory. This is not to say we shouldn't be tolerant and respectful of others but we do not have to agree that their beliefs are correct. Likewise, holding a particular belief is certainly not a licence to condemn or harm others as we will discuss later.

Religion is a product of social and cultural conditioning

Some have claimed that because many of our beliefs are socially and culturally conditioned, no one set of beliefs can be universally true for everyone.

Although living in a certain culture may pre-dispose you towards certain beliefs – it doesn't mean that therefore those beliefs are necessarily true for those people as pluralists claim. Either they are true or not and we need to weigh them objectively regardless of cultural influences.

The irony is that pluralist beliefs – that there is no objective right or wrong for various cultures and that all beliefs are culturally relative - are also culturally relative beliefs. Pluralist beliefs are typically held in Western society but not in other parts of the world due to the Western emphasis on individualism. Social and cultural relativism beliefs are likewise illogical: "All claims about religious beliefs are socially conditioned - except the one I am making right now!"

Bible references

Later in this book, we will be examining evidence as to whether God exists and whether the Bible is trustworthy and reliable. I have used Bible references prior to this where appropriate to show how a particular view is compatible with Christianity. I hope you will forgive me for this. You can of course ignore these verses until we establish the trustworthiness of the Bible.

CHAPTER 2

Scientific Evidence for God

Where did we come from? Examining the cosmos...

Ever looked up on a starry night and wondered where it all came from? How DID the universe (and humanity) come into existence – did God have anything to do with it? What does science say?

Just so we're clear – by universe we mean the totality of existence, including planets, stars, galaxies, the contents of intergalactic space, the smallest subatomic particles, and all matter and energy. This also includes space and time as we know it, which are shaped by matter and energy in the universe and do not exist outside it.[10]

There are only three possibilities of how this mighty and vast universe came into existence.

1. It has always existed (i.e. its eternal)
2. It created itself
3. It was created by something outside itself i.e. God

These options will be explored below.

The Big Bang = A Big Banger?

The first option, that the universe has always been, has been rejected by science due to evidence such as the background radiation echo, the second law of thermodynamics and the motion of the galaxies.

---
10   http://en.wikipedia.org/wiki/Universe

This has led almost all scientists and astronomers to conclude that the universe had a definite starting point known as the 'Big Bang'.

Stephen Hawking, a well-known and highly respected astronomer from Cambridge University states:

> "Almost everyone believes that the universe, and time itself, had a beginning."[11]

Given that the universe had a definite starting point - we are left with the final 2 options – what created or caused this 'Big Bang'. Was it self-created or created by something outside itself?

Did the universe create itself?

The second option – that the universe created itself has been shown to be philosophically impossible.

Before the universe – there was nothing. Nothing cannot create something. How would that be possible? Aristotle had a great definition of nothing: "nothing is what rocks dream about".

If nothing ever existed – nothing could exist now, as nothing cannot create something. For something to exist where nothing did previously – a cause from outside itself is required to create it.

This can be understood with the law of cause and effect which all science is based on stating that every cause has an effect and every effect has a cause.

The universe is also an effect which started with a 'singularity event' and therefore must have a 'cause' for what started this "Big Bang" and the resulting universe.

---

11 Stephen Hawking and Roger Penrose, *The Nature of Space and Time*, The Isaac Newton Institute Series of Lectures (Princeton: Princeton University Press, 1996), p. 20.

Created by God?

We are therefore left with the third option – that something outside of a finite universe (such as God) created it.

So you might be saying – OK if God created the universe, then who created God? However, this assumes God is finite - but at least in the Bible, God is described as eternal. He has always existed and is therefore an 'uncaused cause'.

> Before the mountains were brought forth,
> or ever you had formed the earth and the world,
> from everlasting to everlasting you are God
> (Psalm 90:2, ESV).
>
> Your throne was established long ago; you are from all eternity (Psalm 93:2, NIV).

It is hard for us to grasp the concept of something being eternal - but logically if the universe exists and had a starting point, something must have always existed to create it. Scientist Francis Collins explains:

> "We have this very solid conclusion that the universe had an origin, the Big Bang... the universe began with an unimaginably bright flash of energy from an infinitesimally small point. That implies that before that, there was nothing. I can't imagine how nature, in this case the universe, could have created itself. And the very fact that the universe had a beginning implies that someone was able to begin it. And it seems to be that had to be outside of nature. "[12]

So, although we can't see God, the universe is evidence of His existence. Without God, the universe couldn't exist as there would have been nothing to bring it into being. Just as if we saw a painting or

---

12   Francis S. Collins. (2006). *The Language of God: a Scientist Presents Evidence for Belief.* Simon and Schuster.

a building, we would know there was a painter or builder to create it or 'cause' it to come into being. We wouldn't think it had created itself! And we know the universe (and ourselves) are vastly more complex and magnificent than a painting. Who or what would be capable of creating a universe other than God?

It is far more reasonable to believe that God created the universe, than it created itself. Again, nothing can't create something!

God causing things to exist now?

Not only did God have to cause things to happen in the beginning, He must also still be causing the things you see to exist right now.

It can be argued, some things have causes other than God. For example, a chicken lays an egg. The chicken caused the egg. But then it needs to be asked again - what caused the chicken? There needed to be an egg. We are therefore left with an infinite chicken-egg scenario which is not possible for a finite series which by definition has a beginning and an end. This is like imagining a one-ended stick. We have already established the universe had a beginning – therefore the chicken and egg scenario needs to have a beginning. Therefore, there had to be a beginning cause that created either the chicken or the egg.

Everything in our universe can be considered an 'effect' and therefore must have a cause. This can't go back to infinity; therefore something outside of finite existence must have caused it. Everything that exists now must be made to exist by something else that already exists. Things do not just exist of their own accord. Everything that exists in actuality must have a cause.

Not only did the universe need a cause to get started, it also needs something to give it existence now. The only thing that could explain the existence of things now is something that always existed, had no 'beginning' cause and was infinite and existed outside of time. The logical answer is God!

This can be summarised as follows:

1. Whatever begins to exist must have a cause for its existence
2. The universe began to exist
3. The universe must have a cause for its existence
4. The cause of the universe must exist outside the universe (outside of time) and be eternal (always existed)
5. These are the attributes of God
6. Therefore God caused the universe
7. God exists

The same reasoning can also be applied to anything we see that exists. The cause of all things is God. This concurs with the biblical view:

> He is the radiance of the glory of God and the exact imprint of his nature, and he upholds the universe by the word of his power (Hebrews 1:3, ESV).

If something exists, then God exists

Those who want to make things more complicated may argue, maybe the universe doesn't exist (including ourselves), maybe it is all just an illusion, 'Matrix styles'. In which case, there wouldn't have to be a God who created us and the universe. Although this is an interesting thought, I'm going to hold off from running in front of 'illusory' cars for a while yet. Even if the world was an illusion, we would still have to conclude our 'consciousness' exists, otherwise we wouldn't be thinking about how we came into existence. So we are still left with 'something' that exists, even if it is just our consciousness. Again, something cannot be created from nothing, therefore something eternal must always have existed in order to create something finite.

This thinking - that if something exists, then God must exist - can be dated back to ancient theologians and philosophers such as Plato and St Thomas Aquinas.[13]

The Bible itself points out that the universe is evidence of God. Just as a painting is evidence of a painter or a house the evidence of a builder – creation is evidence of a creator.

> For his invisible attributes, namely, his eternal power and divine nature, have been clearly perceived, ever since the creation of the world, in the things that have been made. So they are without excuse (Romans 1:20).

Do science and the Bible conflict?

Definitely not! As you can see, the discovery of the Big Bang and that the universe had a definite start point provides strong evidence for the existence of a Creator who started this Big Bang. As described in the Bible:

> In the beginning, God created the Heavens and the earth (Genesis 1:1).

In the 20th century, science caught up and confirmed the universe must have a beginning as previously it was believed by many (including Aristotle) to be eternal.

Dr. Arno Penzias who is a Nobel prize winner in physics and co-discoverer of the cosmic microwave background radiation, which helped establish the Big Bang theory of cosmology stated to the New York Times on March 12, 1978:

---

13   http://en.wikipedia.org/wiki/Cosmological_argument

> The best data we have [concerning the Big Bang] are exactly what I would have predicted, had I nothing to go on but the five books of Moses, the Psalms, the Bible as a whole.

In a subsequent radio interview, Penzias was asked what there was before the Big Bang:

> "We don't know, but we can reasonably say that there was nothing." An upset listener called immediately, accusing Penzias of being an atheist. He wisely replied: "Madame, I believe you are not aware of the consequences of what I just said. Before the Big Bang there was nothing of what now exists. Had there been something, the question could be: where did it come from?"

He continued commenting that if there was nothing and suddenly things began to appear, that was a sign that somebody had taken them from nothing, and concluded saying that his discovery could bring about the overcoming of the historic enmity between science and religion.[14]

Conditions for life

As well as the Cosmos, the Big Bang and the law of cause and effect, another compelling argument for the existence of God is the conditions for life. Look around you at creation – isn't it amazing?!?! We've all had our breath taken away by a beautiful sunset or admiring the stars on a clear night.

Not only is it beautiful but the more scientists learn about the universe, the greater it appears to them that conditions on earth have been extremely fine-tuned (designed) to allow life. This is known as the 'Anthropic Principle' and describes the numerous highly unlikely environmental conditions that exist to make life possible on earth.

---

14 Reported by the Discovery Institute, WA, 06-12-07

Numerous conditions needed to fall into an extremely narrow range or 'fine tuning', such as the speed of light, gravity, radiation, nuclear forces, location of the planets and stars etc. to allow for life on earth. The chances of this occurring by chance are so minute - one-in-a-trillion-trillion chance - that they are statistically negligible, meaning there is virtually NO probability of our universe supporting organic and intelligent life by lucky dip.

Stephen Hawking, one of the most respected and well known cosmologists (a non-Christian) says:

> "The universe and the laws of physics seem to have been specifically designed for us. If any of about 40 physical qualities had more than slightly different values, life as we know it could not exist: Either atoms would not be stable, or they wouldn't combine into molecules, or the stars wouldn't form the heavier elements, or the universe would collapse before life could develop, and so on."[15]

John Wheeler, Princeton University professor of physics says:

> "Slight variations in physical laws such as gravity or electromagnetism would make life impossible. The necessity to produce life lies at the center of the universe's whole machinery and design."[16]

The chances of our universe randomly taking its current form as suitable for life have been calculated as one in **10,000,000,000**[124] by Donald Page from Princeton's Institute for Advanced Science. That's one in ten billion to the 124th power – an extraordinarily large number – rendering the chances as virtually impossible of this happening by chance!

---

15 Stephen Hawking, Austin American-Statesman, October 19, 1997
16 John Wheeler, Princeton University, Reader's Digest, September 1986

Scientific Evidence for God

Instead, the 'cosmic welcome mat' that was spread out for us, could surely only be the work of an intelligent creator who intended life to exist on earth? "It's as if the universe knew we were coming" describes scientist Francis Collins:

> "When you look from the perspective of a scientist at the universe, it looks as if it knew we were coming. There are 15 constants – the gravitational constant, various constants about the strong and weak nuclear force etc. – that have precise values. If any one of those constants was off by even one part in a million, or in some cases, by one part in a million million, the universe could not have come to the point where we see it. Matter would not have been able to coalesce, there would have been no galaxy, stars, planets or people."[17]

The only logical conclusion is that there was an intelligent creator behind this.

Atheists and sceptics do not like this conclusion and have come up with an amusing hypothesis of the "multi verse"[18] which speculates that there could be an infinite number of universes hence the chances of one like ours being created is not indicative of God.

There is absolutely no evidence for even one more universe, let alone an infinite number and even if there were millions of universes in addition to our own, atheists are still faced with the difficult question that we dealt with earlier of how THOSE universes came into existence?

As Charlie Campbell amusingly puts it, now "nothing" has not just created one universe, but a lot of universes! It takes a great deal of faith to believe in millions of universes that no one has seen. And even more to believe that "nothing" created them. [19]

---

17   Francis Collins [August 2006 interview with Salon.com]
18   http://en.wikipedia.org/wiki/Multiverse
19   http://www.alwaysbeready.com/god-evidence?id=138

Although it cannot be conclusively proven that the conditions for life in our universe were intentional – the evidence 'beyond reasonable doubt' certainly points to this rather than it being a product of chance.

Intelligent and complex design

Not only does the universe itself reflect intelligent and complex design but every life form on earth reflects this.

All living organisms contain DNA and a single strand of DNA equates to one volume of the Encyclopaedia Britannica! Humans have roughly 100 trillion cells with each cell containing 2 metres of DNA. If you unravelled all of your DNA strands from all of your cells and laid them out end to end, the strands would stretch from the Earth to the Sun hundreds of times. Even bacteria with a single cell are so complex that without all of their parts working together at the same time, they would be unable to survive.[20] It is hard to believe this genetic complexity came into being by chance.

The human body in particular is a marvel to behold. Take a look at your body – your hands and feet, your eyes... So amazingly and intricately designed! If you saw an intricately designed watch – you wouldn't think it had just gotten there by chance – you would know that a lot of thought and planning had gone into the watch and it had to have a designer. The human body and the earth we live in are far more intricate than a watch.

Consider the complexity of the human body, such as brain, skeletal system, muscular system, nervous system and cardiovascular system -all working together to sustain us. The human brain alone contains as much information as the world's largest libraries as described by the late agnostic astronomer Carl Sagan:

---

20 http://www.gotquestions.org/teleological-argument.html

> The information content of the human brain expressed in bits is probably comparable to the total number of connections among the neurons-about a hundred trillion bits [10^{14}]. If written out in English, say, that information would fill some twenty million volumes, as many as in the world's largest libraries... the neurochemistry of the brain is astonishingly busy, the circuitry of a machine more wonderful than any devised by humans. [21]

If we saw a computer, we would never think it had gotten that way by chance – yet the human brain "a machine more wonderful than any devised by humans" – and far more powerful – is considered the product of random evolutionary chance by atheists??

The human heart is also an amazing muscle to consider. Although no bigger than the size of a fist, it keeps blood flowing through 60,000 miles of blood vessels that feed our organs and tissues. It pumps around 75 gallons of blood every hour - around 2000 gallons per day! Each day, our blood travels 12,000 miles courtesy of the heart.[22]

The human eye is another miracle, composed of more than two million working parts, a few of which include lens, retina, cornea, iris, tear glands, eyelashes and finely tuned muscles. It adjusts, lubricates, repairs and cleans itself. It contains 130,000,000 light sensitive rods and cones that convert light into electrical impulses. The eye can make over 100,000 separate motions and can increase its ability to see 100,000 times when it is dark. It transmits signals to the brain at 300 miles per hour.

Dr John Stevens wrote about the eye:

> "..to stimulate 10 milliseconds of the complete processing of even a single nerve cell from the retina would require the solution of 500 simultaneous nonlinear differential equations

---

21 Carl Sagan, *Cosmos*. New York: Random House, 1980, p. 278.
22 http://www.webmd.com/heart-disease/guide/how-heart-works

100 times and would take at least several minutes of processing time on a Cray super computer. Keeping in mind that there are 10 million or more such cells interacting with each other in complex ways, it would take a minimum of 100 years of Cray time to simulate what takes place in your eye many times every second."[23]

We easily recognise intelligent design in our everyday lives. We would not see a car or aeroplane or watch and think they had arrived this way by "chance". A popular illustration often given is the presidential faces carved into Mt Rushmore in South Dakota, USA.[24] Sculpted from a massive granite bluff, this memorial covers around five square kilometres (two square miles). Each head measures approximately 18 metres (60 feet) from forehead to chin — meaning the individual sculptures are twice as high as the head of the Great Sphinx of Giza in Egypt.[25] No one would consider the sculpture to be the product of millions of years of wind and rain, it would indicate an intelligent designer.

Similarly, it is difficult to believe that the human body and brain came into existence without the knowledge and foresight of an intelligent creator. Whilst I'm open to the possibility that the process of evolution could have been used to create the intricate design we now see (more info in part 7), I find it hard to believe that there was not an intelligent designer who foreknew how this process would work and who set it in motion. It is as difficult to believe creation came into being by chance, as it is that far less complex objects such as cars or houses or Mt Rushmore came into being without an intelligent designer.

Of course we cannot know for sure that the complexity and intelligent design reflected in the universe and creation was the foresight of an intelligent designer but it sure looks that way!

---

23   John Stevens, *Byte,* (April 1985, 287-299)
24   http://ncse.com/cej/4/3/scientific-basis-creation-principle-uniformity
25   http://www.answersingenesis.org/articles/cm/v18/n2/mount-rushmore

The Bible states that the earth and humanity is God's handiwork.

> The Heavens declare the glory of God, and the sky above proclaims his handiwork (Psalm 19:1).

> For you formed my inward parts; you knitted me together in my mother's womb. I praise you, for I am fearfully and wonderfully made. Wonderful are your works; my soul knows it very well. My frame was not hidden from you, when I was being made in secret, intricately woven in the depths of the earth. Your eyes saw my unformed substance; in your book were written, every one of them, the days that were formed for me, when as yet there was none of them (Psalm 139:13-16).

Conclusion

We have learnt a lot about whether there is a God from our study of science. Clearly the origins of the universe and the 'Big Bang' provide strong evidence for a creator as it is impossible for 'something' to come from 'nothing'. The conditions required for life and the complexity of design also provide strong evidence for God.

Unless you're prepared to believe the universe originated out of nothing i.e. "the thing rocks dream about" and that once this impossibility occurred, it just magically created the exact conditions for life 'one in a trillion chance' to support organic and human life, then atheism simply isn't a reasonable option! Science certainly supports the existence of God.

CHAPTER 3

Humanistic Evidence for God

As well as science, we can look to humanity and what we observe about ourselves to teach us about the existence of God.

Morality

Most people have strong convictions of right and wrong yet they have never stopped to think about why they have these convictions or where they came from. Every time we argue over right or wrong, we appeal to a higher law that we feel everyone is bound to. Phrases like "it's not fair", "he/she shouldn't treat me like that", "that was dishonest", "I have a right to an opinion" - all appeal to an instinct we have for what is 'right' or 'fair' behaviour and what is unfair, mean or immoral.

Morality is universal with even remote tribes cut off from civilisation observing a code similar to the rest of the worlds. Although differences occur, certain traits are universally revered such as caring for others and truthfulness, while others are looked down on such as greed, selfishness and harming others.[26]

Morality also seems to be innate and is evident in babies. Psychologists observed even 1 year old babies withhold treats from the 'naughty' puppet and give them to the 'good' puppet! [27]

So we observe this strange moral code amongst all humans, where universally people believe things like murder, theft and lying are wrong. Yet, our moral values do not reflect reality in that none of us lives up to this moral code. Where then does this desire for morality

---

26 http://personal.tcu.edu/pwitt/universal%20values.pdf
27 http://www.nytimes.com/2010/05/09/magazine/09babies-t.html?emc=eta1&_r=0

and the moral code come from? The Bible states that it comes from God - the ultimate lawgiver and that all men are aware of the code.

> For when Gentiles [non Jews], who do not have the law, by nature do what the law requires, they are a law to themselves, even though they do not have the law. They show that the work of the law is written on their hearts, while their conscience also bears witness, and their conflicting thoughts accuse or even excuse them (Romans 2:14-15).

In fact, without God, any concept of right and wrong is null and void as there is no 'higher being' or 'judge' to base these convictions on. "Who's to say" whether someone's behaviour is right or wrong? Who's to say Hitler was wrong for exterminating Jews? Without God there is no objective way to decide a moral code or law – this would mean all people and cultures should decide for themselves what is right or wrong and that no one had a right to interfere if a country was mistreating people such as Nazi Germany or terrorist regimes. On what basis could anyone impose their ideas of right or wrong on others if there is no objective moral code? It is simply a matter of preference whether you think something is right or wrong.

Yet we <u>do</u> believe some actions are inherently evil such as infanticide, rape and murder and that the wrongdoer should be punished. We would certainly be upset if our own rights to safety or those of our family were violated.

We also believe in defending human rights and that everyone should be allowed certain rights and freedoms. Why is that? If we're simply random mutations that have evolved from animals, why should people be given special rights? We don't hold animals accountable for killing other animals or not protecting weaker ones.

Morality a product of evolution?

Some contend we have just developed moral tendencies as a survival mechanism. For example, self-sacrificing behaviour towards a tribe or family may result in a greater survival rate for that group. However, in line with this – hostility towards those NOT associated with your people group would also enhance survival. Yet if we saw a total stranger or someone else's child in trouble we would feel morally obligated to help, even if it means putting our own lives in danger. This behaviour would not have been passed down if it were left to 'survival of the fittest' and 'self and clan preservation'.

Others have suggested altruism is a result of social benefits and approval we receive from others. However this does not explain help given when no one knows about it and why we help those in foreign countries by providing aid when we will never meet them.

Again, if we are all a product of chance and morality has just evolved through evolution - "who's to say" whether it's right or wrong to help or harm others? We have no claim to fair treatment and there is no moral obligation to help those in need.

Is moral relativism an option?

Those who try to adopt moral relativism (the belief that all moral law is relative to a culture or person) by saying, "no one should impose their beliefs on others"– still usually believe certain actions are wrong for all people, regardless of race or nationality. Most will agree it is wrong to murder children. Especially it would be wrong to murder THEIR children. They will also certainly react strongly if their rights are in danger of being violated – gun to the head anyone?

Ironically, by making the statement "no one should impose their beliefs on others", the person is in fact imposing a belief about moral relativism on others i.e. the belief that 'no one should impose their beliefs on others'. What makes that particular belief correct and why should everyone else adopt it?

As with all types of relativism, it is logically impossible to be a 'moral relativist' and therefore we need a moral law that transcends humanity, and a universal lawgiver such as God. Even if we were to seriously attempt moral relativism, no one really wants to live in a barbaric world where there is no upholding of justice and no difference between right or wrong.

We all have a conscience and we KNOW some things should not be done regardless of what other people or cultures may say. We also have an innate desire for justice when the rights of ourselves or loved ones have been violated. If there was no right or wrong no one has a right to justice for any suffering.

No such thing as human rights?

The concept of every human being having <u>intrinsic</u> rights against violence and repression is also difficult to uphold without a concept of God. If we are just here by chance, randomly evolving from animals – why would we have any rights at all? Animals commit acts of violence against each other and we don't hold them accountable - what makes it so different when we do it?

If we do agree that human rights are important – who gets to decide what they are? Majority rules through elections and legislation? What if the majority want to oppress the minority? There's also nothing to prevent from legislating AGAINST human rights. There is certainly no basis for us imposing our view of human rights on countries that are causing oppression and violence against their members.

On the other hand, if God exists, then we have a strong case for human rights. If we have all been created in the image of God as the Bible says, then we all have intrinsic value as human beings. We also have something to base laws and morality on – i.e. a higher moral code and law such as that set out in the Bible. It is hard to imagine who would be capable of deciding human rights for humanity other than God himself. In fact the Bible teaches much about morality such as caring for the sick, poor and widows.

We can't deny moral obligation exists, yet without God we can't justify it. However if God DOES exist and He has created us with morality and a sense of right or wrong, then morality makes perfect sense. According to the Bible we live in a fallen world which explains the violence and disorder we see. We were also made for a better world which is why these things bother us.

Denying the existence of God, yet clinging to morality and justice is logically inconsistent. The best we can come up with when holding a 'no God' worldview is that whether murder, theft and rape is wrong is relative to the culture and individual. We can say we 'dislike' it – but not that it's intrinsically right or wrong.

Love, beauty & desire for God

We all know what love and beauty are but without the existence of a God who created us they make no sense. In addition, humans have an innate desire for God and worship – without there actually being a God or gods this also makes no sense.

If we are just here by the product of random chance, with no intelligent creator, then what's the deal with love and beauty? Why do we bother to paint beautiful paintings and create inspiring music? Are they really just hard-wired responses necessary for survival?

It's a bit hard to swallow that the love you feel for others is simply a hard wired response as is your reaction to a beautiful sunset or piece of art or music.

We all desire more than this life offers. We long for love, beauty, meaning and significance. We have an unfulfilled longing for something more and no amount of success, sex, food or relationships will satisfy. Usually the desire for something, indicates it exists. For example, we have an appetite for food because food exists to satisfy that appetite. We have a sexual desire and sex exists to fulfil it. C. S. Lewis puts it well:

> "Creatures are not born with desires unless satisfaction for these desires exists. A baby feels hunger; well, there is such a thing as food. A dolphin wants to swim; well, there is such a thing as water. Men feel sexual desire; well, there is such a thing as sex. If I find in myself a desire which no experience in this world can satisfy, the most probable explanation is that I was made for another world."[28]

Is this because God created us to desire Him with 'a God shaped-hole'? As well as a desire for a better, more satisfying world, described in the Bible as the 'new Earth'?

We can't know for sure but as Timothy Keller puts it:

> "This unfulfillable longing, then qualifies as a deep, innate human desire, and that makes it a major clue that God is there". [29]

The universality of this desire for God and religion points further towards the existence of God. All people groups throughout the world have constructed gods for themselves and the pervasiveness of religion throughout the world is evident.

D.L. Moody wrote:

"Philosophers [have] agreed that even the most primitive races of mankind reach out beyond the world of matter to a superior Being. It

---

28 Lewis, C.S. (2001). *Mere Christianity*. Harper Collins Publishers.
29 Keller, T. (2009). *The Reason for God.* (P.135) London: Hodder & Stoughton

is as natural for man to feel after God as it is for the ivy to feel after a support. Hunger and thirst drive man to seek for food, and there is a hunger of the soul that needs satisfying too. Man does not need to be commanded to worship, as there is not a race so high or so low in the scale of civilization but has some kind of god. What he needs is to be directed aright."

This shows an innate desire for God and a 'deep knowledge' that something exists outside ourselves. It would seem strange indeed that all people throughout history have expressed a desire to worship God if no God actually existed.

No logic without God

We live in a rational world that obeys laws of logic and rationality. Nature is extremely regular with predictable seasons, the sun rises and sets each day, laws of mathematics and gravity work the same today as they did yesterday. This allows us to be able to plan for tomorrow as we know we won't be waking up in a completely different environment.

However without a concept of God, there is no way to account for why such laws of logic or nature should exist. Although atheists can use the laws of logic, they have no way to explain why these laws work or why they exist.

If the laws were man made, different cultures could adopt different laws and rational debate would be impossible. They cannot be simply impulses in the brain as what happens in one person's brain does not necessarily correspond to another person's so there would be no objectivity.

Because the laws of logic are universal and are independent of the material world, they must be based on something unchanging such as a transcendent and immaterial God. Rationality and logic only make sense within a theistic framework.

Life is pointless without God

We all live as if our life matters. We care a lot about the decisions we make, our relationships, jobs, the cars we drive etc. We are all striving to do better, be good people. We live as if the decisions we make are important and that it is better to be kind than to be cruel and that love and beauty are important.

Many people strive after career or professional success and never think about why. To have a few extra toys in this life and then die? If we are here by accident - perhaps randomly evolving from a germ - and there is no God, there is simply no purpose for which we were made. If there is no reason why we are here, why do we live as if our lives matter or have meaning and significance?

If there really is no God – then right or wrong really doesn't matter. If all that exists is this life, then what is it all for? Just to work, sleep, play, live then die? It is all very futile without God. This is the tragic reality for those who deny the existence of God.

Instead we all want to leave a legacy and have our lives count for something. We don't want to believe it is all in vain. The Bible says, "He has put eternity into man's heart" (Ecclesiastes 3:11).

Why do people still cling to the belief of 'no God' but live as if there is one and that this life is important and meaningful? Timothy Keller suggests cynical people may feel this is a way of 'having one's cake and eating it, too'. People can get the benefit of having a God without the cost of following him. However as Keller states, "there is no integrity in that".[30]

The truth will often catch up with people when they stop for a minute and think about the meaning of life and what it is all for – mid-life crisis anyone? It's no surprise depression, anxiety and other mental

---
30 Keller, T. (2009).*The Reason for God.* (P.157) Hodder & Stoughton

disorders are prevalent when faced with the meaninglessness and hopelessness of an existence without God.

Alternatively, you can consider accepting that there IS a God who created us to enjoy love and beauty and with an innate desire for Him. It would provide profound meaning to life and support the belief that human beings have inherent dignity. Morality makes sense when there is a higher being who has given us this sense of right and wrong and who is the ultimate lawgiver and judge.

Conclusion

As well as evidence from science, humanity itself provides clear evidence for God. Our desire for meaning and purpose, love and beauty coupled with a deep 'innate' longing for God as well as the moral law we all acknowledge and adhere to, all points to the existence of a creator. The Big Bang, the fine tuning of the universe, the regularities of nature, logic, love, reason and morality all make perfect sense if God exists. Our lives also have meaning and purpose rather than being the product of chance mutations with no foresight from an intelligent creator.

Even if we deny the existence of God, ironically, we go on living as if He does exist by trusting our sense perceptions, relying on logic and reason and believing love and beauty matter. We live as if our lives matter and have meaning and purpose but the sad reality is that without God they really don't. We are sickened by cruelty and injustice such as child abuse, infanticide, rape and murder. If someone held a gun to our head we would be adamant they are wrong and should be stopped. Yet without a higher moral law giver, we have no intrinsic rights to fair treatment or justice. In short, life and reality as we know it really doesn't make sense without the existence of God.

The combined weight of the scientific and humanistic evidence certainly concludes 'beyond reasonable doubt' that God exists. If this is the case, how do we find out more about this God and which religion if any tells us the truth about God? This will be the focus of Part 2.

PART 2

INVESTIGATING RELIGION & CHRISTIANITY

CHAPTER 4

How To Find Religious Truth

Having concluded 'beyond reasonable doubt' that God exists, let's find out more about Him!

We discussed earlier, the innate desire of humans to worship a god or gods is evidence that a God exists. This desire has led to a plethora of world religions. We established in Chapter 1 that not all religions can be true as they contradict each other and make different claims about the nature of God and reality. This means some must be 'false' religions as per the law of non-contradiction which states that two contradictory statements cannot both be true at the same time (truth will not contradict itself). For example, there cannot be both one God and many gods at the same time.

Our question now becomes: are any of the religions in our world the 'true' religion that will lead us to God? To be valid and considered 'true', any belief system must have the correct world view that lines up with scientific findings, be historically accurate and logical.

False religions

Many religions and world views can be found to be contradictory, irrational or unsupported by historical and scientific evidence.

As discussed earlier, key scientific findings such as the 'Big Bang' prove that the universe had a definite starting point (including all time, space and matter) and therefore needed something outside of time, space and matter to create it. This means we live in a theistic world (belief in the existence of a God or Gods) which rules out Atheism and Naturalism (nothing exists outside the physical world) as valid world views.

Scientific evidence such as the 'Big Bang' has shown us that the universe is NOT eternal and had a definite starting point. Because it had a definite starting point, it needed something outside of it to create it. This rules out all pantheistic worldviews which teach that the universe is God and God is the universe. Pantheistic world views are therefore invalid and includes eastern religions such as Hinduism, Buddhism and Jainism.

Most religions and worldviews are illogical or contradictory. For example, there is no historical evidence to support the book of Mormon. It also teaches a logical impossibility of an infinite regression of gods being formed, that is, each god was made a god by a previous god as far back as infinity. However, it is impossible to cross an infinite number of each god becoming a god in order to get to the present time. An infinite period of time cannot be crossed as otherwise it isn't infinite. Therefore, there cannot be an infinite regression of new gods being formed, meaning Mormonism is false.[31]

Islam's book of Quran claims to be a perfect book preserved on tablets in Heaven, yet contains both contradictions and errors. For example, it teaches a man's seed comes from his chest – not his testicles (Quran 86:5-7). It describes crucifixion before its invention (Quran 7:123-124) and says that birds and ants can talk (27:16; 27:18)[32]. Contradictions include claiming four different ways man was created – by blood, clay, dust and nothing.[33]

1. "Created man, out of a (mere) clot of congealed blood" (96:2).

2. "We created man from sounding clay, from mud moulded into shape" (15:26).

3. "The similitude of Jesus before Allah is as that of Adam; He created him from dust, then said to him: "Be". And he was" (3:59).

---

31 http://carm.org/logical-proof-that-mormonism-is-false
32 http://carm.org/how-do-we-know-christianity-true-and-we-are-not-deceived
33 http://carm.org/contradictions-quran

4. "But does not man call to mind that We created him before out of nothing?" (19:67, Yusuf Ali). Also, 52:35).

Therefore we can conclude Islam is false. It will be further considered in contrast to the claims of Christianity which we will investigate in following chapters.

Whilst time doesn't allow for the analysis of every religion, suffice to say, the majority of religions and belief systems can be found false in this way.

True religion

To find religious truth, we can look to our previous study of science and humanity to find answers about who God really is and whether this corresponds with any religious claims.

So far we have learnt that God is:[34]

- Supernatural – exists outside of creation
- Powerful – created the universe
- Eternal – exists outside of time and space
- Omnipresent & immaterial – not limited by time or space as exists outside of it
- Timeless and unchanging – he created time
- Infinite and a single being – can't have two infinite beings
- Intelligent – to create the universe
- Moral – created the moral law
- Caring – gave us the moral law to stop us hurting ourselves and others

---

[34] Read more: http://www.gotquestions.org/correct-religion.html#ixzz33pypFocM

- Personal – wants us to know him & created a desire within us for Himself

This God shows characteristics that are described by the God of Judaism, Islam and Christianity. These are the only major faiths remaining after eliminating pantheistic religions and the atheistic worldview.

While we can learn some things about God from science, logic and human nature, we can't learn everything. To learn more about God, we need God to reveal himself to us.

Judaism, Islam and Christianity all claim to have a book that is God's revelation to man. The main differences between these religions (and their corresponding books) are whether the New Testament is true and whether Jesus was God or man. Islam and Judaism both say that the New Testament claims are untrue and that Jesus was not the son of God.

Investigating Christianity

Three religions, Judaism, Islam and Christianity could be considered valid based on the evidence so far.

As discussed, the major difference between these are whether the New Testament claims of Christianity – that Jesus was the Son of God are true or not. This will now be the focal point of our investigation. We will look at historical and archaeological evidence for the Bible, the New Testament and Jesus. We will investigate whether there is evidence for:

1. The accuracy of the Bible as a whole
2. The validity and accuracy of the New Testament

3. New Testament claims that Jesus was the Son of God

4. Jesus being crucified and rising from the dead and other miracles

We will also look at objections to God, the Bible and Christianity.

We will then assess the evidence and see what we can conclude about God and Christianity.

CHAPTER 5

The Bible & New Testament – True or False?

Christians believe the Bible is God's revelation to man.

However, many people believe the Bible cannot be trusted either historically, or as the Word of God. This view has been amplified by best-selling novels such as The Da Vinci Code. Whilst The Da Vinci Code received much criticism as most of the alleged 'facts' were either incorrect or had little or no support, doubts continue to be raised about whether the Bible is trustworthy. 'The Jesus Seminar' is another example of an organisation that seeks to shed doubt that the gospels are historically accurate.[35]

Can we trust the New Testament gospels?

The New Testament clearly depicts that Jesus is the Son of God and that He was crucified on a cross in order to reconcile sinful humanity with a Holy God. It teaches that He rose after three days, conquering sin and death and appeared to many witnesses. These events are recorded in the New Testament and are the basis of the Christian faith. The question for modern Bible readers is, "can the New Testament be trusted as a historical and true record of events or are the events simply legends with made up stories of Jesus performing many miracles and rising from the dead?"

The 'canonical' gospels of the New Testament that the church has accepted as genuine includes Matthew, Mark, Luke & John. It is often claimed the New Testament Gospels were written so many years after the events happened, that the writers' accounts can't be trusted and are

---

35 http://en.wikipedia.org/wiki/Jesus_Seminar

closer to being 'legends' than the truth. Books like The Da Vinci Code have popularised the acceptance of alternative gospels including the 'Gnostic gospels' which depict Jesus as merely human. The claim is these Gnostic gospels were suppressed by political and church bodies whom wanted Jesus to appear deified. We will now investigate these claims and the trustworthiness of the New Testament gospels.

Timing too early for gospels to be legends

The canonical gospels were written at the very most forty to sixty years after Jesus' death. Paul's letters were written fifteen to twenty five years after the death of Jesus – this means that many who witnessed the events were still alive. The gospel author Luke says that he got his account of Jesus' life from eye witnesses who were still alive (Luke 1:1-4) – which he couldn't have written unless it was true and could be verified.

Richard Bauckham in his book *Jesus and the Eyewitnesses* uses historical evidence to show there were many eye witnesses still alive when the gospels were written. Active members of the church community had committed these accounts to memory and could verify the truth of the Canonised Gospel accounts.[36] The Gospel writers named the eyewitnesses in the text who could verify the accounts at any time. For example, in the Gospel of Mark, the man who helped Jesus carry his cross to Calvary 'was the father of Alexander and Rufus' (Mark 15:21).

Paul also claims there were over 500 witnesses who saw Jesus. It would have been impossible for Paul to write this unless there really were a large number of witnesses who could confirm the events.

> For I delivered to you as of first importance what I also received: that Christ died for our sins in accordance with the

---

[36] Keller, T. (2009). *The Reason for God.* (P.101) Hodder & Stoughton

Scriptures, that he was buried, that he was raised on the third day in accordance with the Scriptures, and that he appeared to Cephas, then to the twelve. Then he appeared to more than five hundred brothers at one time, most of whom are still alive, though some have fallen asleep. (1 Corinthians 15:3-6)

This provides clear evidence for the Gospel accounts as historical fact with living eyewitnesses, rather than loosely formed stories passed from one person to the next. Officials and opponents of Jesus were also still alive at the time of writing and would have been highly motivated to challenge any false accounts.

For a largely altered fictional account to be published it would be necessary for all eyewitnesses along with their close relatives and children to be dead so they could not contradict the accounts. The gospels were written too soon after the events for this to be the case.

The new faith would not have spread as it did had Jesus not done the things mentioned in the Gospel accounts. Paul confidently asserts to King Agrippa "These things were not done in a corner" (Acts 26:26) – he was referring to the fact that tens of thousands of people had heard and seen Jesus and that what he had done was public knowledge.

In contrast, leading New Testament scholar NT Wright dates the Gospel of Thomas, one of the "Gnostic gospels" as being put together nearly 200 years after the time of Jesus.[37] The idea of Emperor Constantine destroying earlier Gnostic gospels that depicted Jesus as just a human teacher as alleged in The Da Vinci Code is simply untrue. Typically Gnostic Christianity portrayed Jesus as LESS human than orthodox Christianity. Many Gnostic sects considered Christ purely divine as they considered matter evil and contended that a divine sprit would never take on a material body.[38]

---

37 http://www.spu.edu/depts/uc/response/summer2k5/features/davincicode.asp
38 http://en.wikipedia.org/wiki/Criticism_of_The_Da_Vinci_Code

Honest accounts

Some claim the gospels were written by early church leaders to promote their own agenda. However, this does not fit with the actual content. Rather than content that would promote Christianity or church agenda – the New Testament instead honestly depicts the authors and characters failings and weaknesses of the disciples and local church. The accounts even include times of Jesus' weaknesses, such as crying in grief for a loved one or in agony of soul. Much of the content is counterproductive to promoting Christianity and its leaders.

For example, one of the church disputes was over whether gentile Christians (non Jews) should be circumcised. If the content was fabricated, they could easily have inserted Jesus' 'viewpoint' on the topic, however none is presented – indicating the church leaders did not deem it appropriate to alter the accounts.[39]

Also, anyone who was crucified was assumed to be a criminal – therefore it seems unlikely that leaders of the early Christian movement who wanted to promote Jesus as divine would have fabricated this as it would have cast doubt on His character. Similarly, the story of Jesus in the garden of Gethsemane where He is in agony of soul foreknowing the need to go to the cross, as well as crying out on the cross that God had abandoned Him, would have made Him appear weak and afraid.

Depicting women as the first eye witnesses of the resurrection would also have been a poor move for a fabricated story as women were of such low status their testimony was not admissible evidence in court. A better strategy would have been to state that male pillars of the community had witnessed these incidents. The only reasonable explanation is because this is the actual way the events transpired.

The apostles are often depicted as foolish, squabbling and cowardly, such as when they are arguing over 'who is the greatest' (Luke 9:46)

---

[39] Keller, T. (2009). *The Reason for God.* Hodder & Stoughton

or when Peter denies knowing Jesus (Mark 14:71). Only Peter himself could have been the proponent of this story and it is unlikely someone would make up a story of themselves looking cowardly.

The disciples are also described as 'falling asleep' several times when Jesus, in His hour of greatest need had asked them to pray (Matthew 26:36-46). They all abandoned Him when He was arrested (Mark 14:50). If the disciples had simply made up this story they would have surely depicted themselves as heroic and faithful to Jesus. To further the gospel for political or social ends, it would have been wiser to display the apostles leading the church as wise and courageous.

The canonical gospels with their emphasis on helping the poor also greatly offended the Greek and Roman leaders.

In contrast the 'Gnostic gospels' contain content that is more in line with what the political leaders of the time would have wanted to promote.

Detailed accounts

The narratives contain much detail which was not the style of ancient fiction. Today's fiction contains much detail to make it seem realistic, however this was not how fiction was written at the time the Gospels were penned. Details were only included if they related to character or plot development.[40]

C.S. Lewis who was a well-known literary scholar and critic notes:

> "I have been reading poems, romances, vision literature, legends and myths all my life. I know what they are like. I know none of them are like this. Of this text there are only two possible views. Either this is reportage… or else, some unknown writer… without known predecessors or successors, suddenly anticipated the whole technique of modern novelistic,

---
40 Keller, T. (2009).*The Reason for God.* London: Hodder & Stoughton

realistic narrative...".[41]

Instead the narratives are in the style of eyewitness historical accounts.

Reliable eyewitnesses

'Cold Case Christianity' by J. Warner Wallace is a fascinating account of how a homicide detective applied his investigative skills to determine whether the claims of Christianity are true and in particular the validity of the gospels as eye witness accounts. Detective Jim Wallace scrutinised the gospels and applied the same rigorous tests he places witnesses and suspects through to investigate crimes. He carefully explained the methods he used as a detective, then applied these same methods to assess the reliability of the four gospels as eyewitness accounts of history. He concluded 'beyond reasonable doubt' the New Testament accounts are highly reliable and he was subsequently converted from atheism to Christianity.

Cold Case Christianity is recommended reading for anyone who is interested.

Rigorous tests for inclusion

The 27 New Testament books went through a rigorous process before being formally included in the Bible in 397AD by the Council of Carthage. This process is referred to as the 'canonisation' of scripture. Scholars believe the criteria used were:[42]

- Apostolic – This was the main criteria – that the book was written by an apostle or a close companion of one.

- Universal acceptance – Widely accepted by the majority of

---

41   C.S. Lewis, Christian Reflections, Walter Hooper, ed. (Eerdmans, 1967), p.155 cited at Keller, T. (2009).The Reason for God. London: Hodder & Stoughton
42   http://en.wikipedia.org/wiki/Development_of_the_New_Testament_canon

churches

- Orthodox – Agreed with accepted and approved teachings and theology of other Christian writings
- Holy Spirit – The church authorities felt the inner witness of the Holy Spirit in selecting certain books

Although ultimately God decided which books to include, we can be sure they also went through a rigorous human process and that there are no additional books that should be there or ones that are included that didn't meet the strict requirements.

The disciples persecution

In accordance with the events recorded in the New Testament, the disciples endured great persecution for proclaiming that Jesus was the Son of God and had risen from the dead.

The apostle Paul is a well-known example. Born into the privileged position with all the rights of Roman citizenship as well as holding the highly regarded position of Pharisee, Paul relinquished this and suffered much persecution. Paul eventually died a martyr's death for his belief in Christ. An account of his credentials and persecution as described in the Bible:

> If anyone else thinks he has reason for confidence in the flesh, I have more: circumcised on the eighth day, of the people of Israel, of the tribe of Benjamin, a Hebrew of Hebrews; as to the law, a Pharisee; as to zeal, a persecutor of the church; as to righteousness under the law, blameless. But whatever gain I had, I counted as loss for the sake of Christ. Indeed, I count everything as loss because of the surpassing worth of knowing Christ Jesus my Lord. For his sake I have suffered the loss of all things and count them as rubbish, in order that I may gain

Christ (Philippians 3:4-8).

Are they servants of Christ? I am a better one—I am talking like a madman—with far greater labors, far more imprisonments, with countless beatings, and often near death. Five times I received at the hands of the Jews the forty lashes less one. Three times I was beaten with rods. Once I was stoned. Three times I was shipwrecked; a night and a day I was adrift at sea; on frequent journeys, in danger from rivers, danger from robbers, danger from my own people, danger from Gentiles, danger in the city, danger in the wilderness, danger at sea, danger from false brothers; in toil and hardship, through many a sleepless night, in hunger and thirst, often without food, in cold and exposure. And, apart from other things, there is the daily pressure on me of my anxiety for all the churches (2 Corinthians 11:23-28).

Many more of the early Christians were also imprisoned, beaten and stoned to death for declaring their beliefs about Jesus.

About that time Herod the king laid violent hands on some who belonged to the church. He killed James the brother of John with the sword, and when he saw that it pleased the Jews, he proceeded to arrest Peter also (Acts 12:1-3).

The New Testament only records events from the birth of Jesus Christ though until the time Paul and the apostles were travelling around Rome, preaching about Christ, so doesn't record the death of all the apostles. However, sources outside the Bible record their deaths and it is believed that all the apostles except John were martyred for their beliefs.

Example from Josephus, the first century historian:

"Festus was now dead, and Albinus was but upon the road; so he assembled the Sanhedrim of judges, and brought before them the brother of Jesus, who was called Christ, whose name was James, and some others, [or, some of his companions]; and when he had formed an accusation against them as breakers of the law, he delivered them to be stoned…"

The Antiquities of the Jews — Flavius Josephus

Bartholomew was martyred by King Astyages in Armedia:

"And when he had thus spoken, the king was informed that this god Baldad and all the other idols had fallen down, and were broken in pieces. Then the king rent the purple in which he was clothed, and ordered the holy apostle Bartholomew to be beaten with rods; and after having been thus scourged, to be beheaded." - Martyrdom of Bartholomew.

This goes against those who claim the disciples were lying and merely pretending Jesus rose from the dead. Not only did they have no possible motive for doing this but they had every motive to say exactly the opposite. It is one thing to die for something you 'think' is true, as in the case of terrorist bombers today but no one is willing to die for something they KNOW is a lie. The disciples did not recant their testimony that they had seen Jesus and that He had risen from the dead. Unlike terrorist bombers, the disciples had seen Jesus with their own eyes and no amount of beating or torture made them go back on their testimony. It's hard to believe that people would be prepared to die defending something they knew was a lie.

Archaeological evidence

Archaeological discoveries have confirmed the people, places and events described by the Bible to be historically accurate.

Nelson Glueck, a well-known archaeologist, who has been featured in Time Magazine and is one of the pioneers of Bible archaeology stated:

"It may be stated categorically that no archaeological discovery has ever controverted a Biblical reference. Scores of archaeological findings have been made which confirm in clear outline or exact detail historical statements in the Bible. And, by the same token, proper evaluation of Biblical descriptions has often led to amazing discoveries." - Nelson Glueck[43]

The examples below can give us confidence that the authors were reporting events that actually happened rather than constructing fanciful stories to trick or deceive.

1. Pontius Pilot

Pontius Pilot is described in the New Testament as overseeing Jesus' trial and sentencing him to death (Matthew 27:2; Luke 3:1).

Archaeologists have confirmed he was a real historical person with the discovery of a limestone block with the inscription "Pontius Pilot, Prefect of Judea" which also confirms the position ascribed to him in the Gospel accounts. Since then, Pilate's official residence at Caesarea has also been identified.[44]

2. Caiaphas

Caiaphas is described as the Jewish High Priest who questioned Jesus regarding His deity. When Jesus answered, Caiaphas accused Him of blasphemy, resulting in Jesus' condemnation (Matthew 26:3, Matthew 26:57–68).

Archaeologists found a very ornate bone burial box with an inscription "Joseph, son of Caiaphas."

Whilst the gospel writers refer to him as 'Caiaphas', Josephus

---

43 Dr. Nelson Glueck, *Rivers in the Desert,* (New York: Farrar, Strous and Cudahy, 1959), 136
44 http://www.alwaysbeready.com/Bible-evidence?id=99

an ancient 1st century historian tells us his full name was 'Joseph Caiaphas'.[45]

3. David

It wasn't until 1993 that evidence was found outside the Bible for the existence of King David of Israel. Prior to then people were prone to dismiss stories about him as mythological.[46]

Supporting the existence of King David, an Aramean victory stone was discovered at the town of Dan in Israel describing the defeat of the Kings of Judah and Israel and contains the phrases 'the King of Israel' and the 'House of David'.[47]

U. S. News & World Report religion writer, Jeffery Sheler, said:

> "The fragmentary reference to David was a historical bombshell. Never before had the familiar name of Judah's ancient warrior king, a central figure of the Hebrew Bible and, according to Christian Scripture, an ancestor of Jesus, been found in the records of antiquity outside the pages of the Bible. Sceptical scholars had long seized upon that fact to argue that David was a mere legend...Now, at last, there was material evidence, an inscription written not by Hebrew scribes but by an enemy of the Israelites a little more than a century after David's presumptive lifetime. It seemed to be a clear corroboration of the existence of King David's dynasty and, by implication, of David himself." [Sheler, Is the Bible True? 60–61.][48]

---

45 http://en.wikipedia.org/wiki/Caiaphas
46 http://www.alwaysbeready.com/Bible-evidence?id=99
47 http://en.wikipedia.org/wiki/David
48 http://www.alwaysbeready.com/Bible-evidence?id=99

Whilst there is much archaeological evidence to support the Bible, no archaeological evidence has been found to support any other religious books.

Extra biblical writings

There are many writings outside the Bible that verify the historical accuracy of the Bible. These sources verify that 50 persons mentioned in the Old Testament and 30 persons in the New Testament were real historical figures.[49]

The details of Jesus' life have been confirmed by more than 30 sources outside the Bible concerning his life, death, teachings and resurrection.[50] One of these includes first century historian Flavius Josephus[51]. Josephus mentions many people written about in the Bible including Herod the Great, Herod Antipas, Caiaphas, Pontius Pilate, John the Baptist, James "the brother of Jesus," Felix, Festus, and Jesus himself.[52]

One of Josephus' statements about Jesus includes:

"At this time there was a wise man who was called Jesus. And his conduct was good, and (he) was known to be virtuous. And many people from among the Jews and the other nations became his disciples. Pilate condemned him to be crucified to die. And those who had become his disciples did not abandon his discipleship. They reported that he had appeared to them three days after his crucifixion and that he was alive..."[53]

49 Geisler, N. & Turek, F. (2004).*I Don't Have Enough Faith To Be An Atheist.* Crossway.
50 Gary R. Habermas (1996)*The Historical Jesus: Ancient Evidence for the Life of Christ.* College Press Publishing(http://www.alwaysbeready.com/Bible-evidence?id=99)
51 http://en.wikipedia.org/wiki/Josephus
52 http://www.alwaysbeready.com/Bible-evidence?id=99
53 Antiquities of the Jews, 18:63-64, from a surviving manuscript in Arabic

The Bible & New Testament – True or False?

Other historians also mention and corroborate details in the Old Testament. Charlie Campbell discusses this in more detail in his book "Archaeological Evidence for the Bible".

Manuscript evidence

The New Testament manuscripts are more numerous and more well preserved than for any other ancient writing such as Plato, Aristotle and Homer as demonstrated in the chart below[54]. There are over 5,800 complete or fragmented Greek manuscripts, 10,000 Latin manuscripts and 9,300 manuscripts from other ancient languages.[55] This means they can be cross checked for accuracy and have been found to be 99% textually pure. With such a large number of copies, there are many thousands of accidental errors made by scribes such as an omitted word, a duplicate line, a misspelling, a rearrangement of words, however these are easily identified as such. A vast number of copies means it is easy to identify any major deviations or errors. Some variations involve apparently intentional changes, which often make more difficult a determination of whether they were corrections from better exemplars, harmonisations between readings, or ideologically motivated.

Author	Date Written	Earliest Copy	Approximate Time Span between original & copy	Number of Copies	Accuracy of Copies
Lucretius	died 55 or 53 B.C.		1100 yrs	2	----
Pliny	A.D. 61-113	A.D. 850	750 yrs	7	----
Plato	427-347 B.C.	A.D. 900	1200 yrs	7	----
Demosthenes	4th Cent. B.C.	A.D. 1100	800 yrs	8	----
Herodotus	480-425 B.C.	A.D. 900	1300 yrs	8	----

54 http://carm.org/manuscript-evidence
55 http://en.wikipedia.org/wiki/Biblical_manuscript

Author	Date Written	Earliest Copy	Approximate Time Span between original & copy	Number of Copies	Accuracy of Copies
Suetonius	A.D. 75-160	A.D. 950	800 yrs	8	----
Thucydides	460-400 B.C.	A.D. 900	1300 yrs	8	----
Euripides	480-406 B.C.	A.D. 1100	1300 yrs	9	----
Aristophanes	450-385 B.C.	A.D. 900	1200	10	----
Caesar	100-44 B.C.	A.D. 900	1000	10	----
Livy	59 BC-AD 17	----	???	20	----
Tacitus	circa A.D. 100	A.D. 1100	1000 yrs	20	----
Aristotle	384-322 B.C.	A.D. 1100	1400	49	----
Sophocles	496-406 B.C.	A.D. 1000	1400 yrs	193	----
Homer (Iliad)	900 B.C.	400 B.C.	500 yrs	643	95%
New Testament	1st Cent. A.D. (A.D. 50-100)	2nd Cent. A.D. (c. A.D. 130 f.)	less than 100 years	5600	99.50%

Scholars agree the New Testament books appear to have been written during the 1st century – within 70 years of Jesus crucifixion. This means there would have been many living witnesses at the time they were written who would have contested any inaccuracies. Fragments of the book of John have been dated only 125-160 AD leaving only a very short time span between the original and the copy. This is in contrast to other ancient writings which have many hundreds of years between the original and the copy.

The discovery of the Dead Sea Scrolls in 1947 in Qumran, east of Jerusalem on the shore of the Dead Sea, provided great support to the accuracy of the Old Testament. A young shepherd discovered the ceramic pots containing the scrolls whilst following a goat that had gone astray. After much searching, tens of thousands of scroll fragments were found dating from the third century BC to AD 68. This included every book of the Hebrew Bible except the Book of Esther as well as other religious and non-religious works. These were older than any manuscripts previously discovered, yet there were minimal differences in previous manuscripts, demonstrating the Bible we have today is the same Bible that the early church possessed 2,000 years ago.

Fulfilled prophecy

The Bible is the only religious book containing fulfilled prophecy. The Bible contains over three hundred specific and detailed prophecies written hundreds of years before they came to pass.[56]

Prophecy about Jesus	Old Testament Prophecy	New Testament Fulfilment
Born of a virgin	Isaiah 7:14	Matt. 1:18, 25
Born at Bethlehem	Micah 5:2	Matt. 2:1
He would be preceded by a Messenger	Isaiah 40:3	Matt. 3:1-2
He would heal the blind, deaf and lame	Isaiah 35:5-6	Matthew 11:5
Rejected by His own people	Isaiah 53:3, Psalm 118:22	John 7:5; 7:48, 1 Peter 2:7
Betrayed by a close friend	Psalm 41:9	John 13:26-30
His side pierced	Zech. 12:10	John 19:34
He would be crucified	Psalm 22:1, Zechariah 12:10	Luke 23:33;
	Psalm 22:11-18	John 19:23-24
Resurrection of Christ	Psalm 16:10	Acts 13:34-37

---

56 http://www.accordingtothescriptures.org/prophecy/353prophecies.html

With such a long time span, there is no way the writers could have known these details about Jesus unless God had guided their writing. Some may claim that the New Testament was fabricated to make it look as if Jesus fulfilled Old Testament prophecy - however there is absolutely no evidence for this. We have also discussed the extreme unlikelihood that Jesus' disciples would have been prepared to die for lies they had made up about Jesus being the Messiah.

There is no other religion or worldview that demonstrates fulfilled prophecy as Christianity does.

The Bible's internal consistency

The Bible addresses many of life's most difficult questions about our existence, God, our purpose, good and evil, as well as death in a clear and consistent manner.

This is astounding considering as Charlie Campbell has noted:[57]

- The Bible is comprised of 66 different documents
- The Bible was written by approximately 40 different authors from various educational and cultural backgrounds
- Was written over a period of 1500+ years so many of the authors didn't know each other
- Many of the authors were located hundreds of miles apart
- Was written in three different languages: Hebrew, Aramaic and Greek
- The Bible never deviates from its consistent message that God is seeking to reconcile sinful humanity to himself though His son, Jesus Christ.

---

57   http://www.alwaysbeready.com/Bible-evidence?id=99

Jesus' assurance

Jesus also assured us the Bible was the Word of God and to be trusted.

> Sanctify them in the truth; your word is truth (John 17:17).

He frequently quoted the Bible and used it when being tempted to defeat Satan (Mathew 4:4-10).

> He claimed it could not be broken or destroyed.

> If he called them gods to whom the word of God came—and Scripture cannot be broken—(John 10:35)

> For truly, I say to you, until Heaven and earth pass away, not an iota, not a dot, will pass from the Law until all is accomplished (Matthew 5:18).

The New Testament is also inspired by God as Jesus promised the Holy Spirit would help the disciples remember what He said and would declare things to come.

> But the Helper, the Holy Spirit, whom the Father will send in my name, he will teach you all things and bring to your remembrance all that I have said to you (John 14:26).

> When the Spirit of truth comes, he will guide you into all the truth, for he will not speak on his own authority, but whatever he hears he will speak, and he will declare to you the things that are to come (John 16:13).

There is much historical evidence including extrabiblical writings that Jesus was a real person, who performed the miracles described in the Bible and then died and rose again. His Word on these matters can be trusted.

The Bible's ability to transform lives

The Bible claims to be living, active and enlightening.

> For the word of God is living and active, sharper than any two-edged sword, piercing to the division of soul and of spirit, of joints and of marrow, and discerning the thoughts and intentions of the heart (Hebrews 4:12).

> Your word is a lamp to my feet and a light to my path (Psalm 119:105).

It has changed lives and impacted societies like no other book. From the Ten Commandments, which form the basis of many of our laws, to the Golden Rule, family values, education, as well as many Bible phrases commonly used today, it has greatly influenced western society and individual lives.

Wherever Biblical Truths have been preached and been received, it has transformed lives and converted many sinners to belief in Jesus Christ. Millions of sinners, including myself, have had their lives turned around from things like drugs, prostitution, alcoholism, addictions, loneliness, depression and more to become godly men and women as they have studied the Bible. They have found meaning and purpose within its pages and discovered who they are in Christ.

Among other things, the Bible has inspired people to:

- Build hospitals and orphanages
- Build universities (Harvard, Yale & Princeton were started by Christians for Christian teaching)
- Humanitarian efforts to help the poor
- Labour for human rights and equality

Conclusion

We have discussed copious evidence for the validity of the Bible and the New Testament events that claim that Jesus was the son of God including:

- The short time period that the gospels were written after Jesus' death, meaning fictional accounts could have been easily disputed by witnesses as well as opponents to Christianity

- 500+ eyewitnesses to Jesus' resurrection who could confirm or deny the events

- Honest, reliable accounts which don't attempt to hide or omit unflattering or problematic details

- The New Testament was written by nine different authors who all corroborate that Jesus was God

- The disciples' persecution – they did not recant their testimony of Jesus rising from the dead even when faced with torture and death

- Previously cowardly apostles who were willing to die for testifying that Jesus rose from the dead

- Archaeological evidence supports people and places mentioned in the bible

- Historical, non-biblical writings record the life of Jesus and His disciples

- The huge volume of manuscripts, accurately transmitted through the centuries

- Internal consistency of the Bible despite being written over a period of 1500+ years by 40 different authors, often living hundreds of miles apart.

- The Bible's ability to transform lives

From this we can conclude that the New Testament represents accurate eye witness testimonies that confirm Jesus was the Son of God. If Jesus IS God, then what He says about the Bible must be true. Jesus says it is inerrant, unchanging and unbreakable and inspired by God.[58] We can safely conclude the Bible and New Testament are true and are God's word to humanity.

Therefore, any teachings of Islam or Judaism that contradict the Bible cannot be true. Since they both reject Jesus as God in human form, they are false religions. Since we can know God through the Bible and Jesus, all forms of agnosticism (that God can't be known or is unknowable) are refuted. As well as Biblical and historical proof, there is further evidence Jesus is the Son of God which we will now explore.

---

[58] Matthew 5:17 – 19, Luke 16:17, John 10:35, 2 Timothy 3:16.

CHAPTER 6

Evidence Jesus is God

We have discussed a great deal of evidence supporting the Bible as an honest and historical account of Jesus life. There is also special evidence that Jesus is the son of God and not a 'wise teacher' or 'prophet'. This is by way of fulfilled prophecy and miracles - the greatest of which was the resurrection of Christ.

Fulfilled prophecy

We discussed earlier that the hundreds of fulfilled prophecies about Jesus provides strong evidence that the Bible is inspired by God. With the Old Testament prophecies written hundreds of years before their fulfilment, there is no way the writers could have known the details, unless they were inspired by God.

Another main purpose of prophecy was for ancient and modern people to recognise Jesus as the Messiah and provide proof of His claims to be the Son of God.

Peter Stoner, author of Science Speaks took just 8 of the many prophecies about Jesus and calculated the probability of a single man fulfilling these. He had his students discuss at length each prophecy and conditions which might affect the probability of any man (Jesus or otherwise) fulfilling it. After discussion, the students agreed unanimously on estimates that were both reasonable and extremely conservative as listed on the following page.[59]

---

59 (http://www.goodnewsdispatch.org/math.html)

Old Testament Prophecy	New Testament Fulfilment	Probability
Christ to be born in Bethlehem	And Herod asked where Christ had been born ... they answered Bethlehem	2.8×10^5 or 1 in 280,000
(Micah 5:2)	(Matt 2:4-6)	
Forerunner of Christ	John the Baptist, the forerunner of Christ	1×10^3 or 1 in 1,000
(Malachi 3:1)	(Mark 1:2-8)	
Christ to enter Jerusalem riding on a donkey	Christ enters Jerusalem riding on a donkey	1×10^2 or 1 in 100
(Zech 9:9)	(Matt 21:4-11)	
Christ to be betrayed by a friend	Judas betrayed Jesus	1×10^3 or 1 in 1,000
(Psalm 41:9)	(Luke 22:21)	
Christ to be betrayed for 30 pieces of silver	Judas sold out Jesus for 30 pieces of silver	1×10^3 or 1 in 1,000
(Zech 11:12)	(Matt 26:15)	
30 pieces of silver casted down and used to buy a potter's field	30 pieces of silver used to buy a potter's field	1×10^5 or 1 in 100,000
(Zech 11:13)	(Matt 27:3-10)	
Although innocent, Christ kept silent when on trial	Jesus kept silent when questioned	1×10^3 or 1 in 1,000
(Isaiah 53:7)	(Mark 14:60-61)	
Christ crucified	Jesus was crucified	1×10^4 or 1 in 10,000
(Psalm 22:16)	(John 19:17, 18)	

They calculated the chance that any man might have lived down to the present time and fulfilled all eight prophecies as 1 in 10^{17} which is 1 in 100,000,000,000,000,000. The prophecies were either given by inspiration of God or the prophets had just one chance in 10^{17} of having them come true in any man, but they all came true in Christ.

Stoner illustrates this extremely rare chance by supposing that "we take 10^{17} silver dollars and lay them on the face of Texas. They will cover all of the state two feet deep. Now mark one of these silver dollars and stir the whole mass thoroughly, all over the state... Blindfold a man and tell him that he can travel as far as he wishes, but he must pick up one silver dollar and say that this is the right one. What chance would he have of getting the right one? Just the same chance that the prophets would have had of writing these eight prophecies and having them all come true in any one man."[60]

Stoner then considers the chances of fulfilling 48 prophecies and says, "we find the chance that any one man fulfilled all 48 prophecies to be 1 in 10^{157}, or 1 in

100,000,000,000,000,000,000,000,000,000,000,000,000,000,000,000,000,000,000,000,000,000,000,000,000,000,000,000,000,000,000,000,000,000,000, 000, 000,000,000,000,000,000,000,000,000,000,000,000,000.

This is astonishing proof of Jesus deity. Clearly, He did not fulfil these prophecies by accident!

Miracles

Jesus made some astonishing claims that He was the son of God. Anyone could claim this - but Jesus backed up His claims to divinity with evidence. No other person in history has performed the miracles Jesus did including:[61]

---

60 http://sciencespeaks.dstoner.net/Christ_of_Prophecy.html#ca
61 http://carm.org/why-believe-christianity-over-all-other-religions

- Turned water into wine (John 2:6-10).
- Cast out demons (Matt. 8:28-32; 15:22-28).
- Healed lepers (Matt. 8:3; Luke 17:14).
- Healed diseases (Matt. 4:23, 24; Luke 6:17-19).
- Healed a paralytic (Mark 2:3-12).
- Raised the dead (Matt. 9:25; John 11:43-44).
- Restored sight to the blind (Matt. 9:27-30; John 9:1-7).
- Fed thousands with five loaves and two fish (Matt. 14:15-21; Matt. 15:32-38).
- Walked on water (Matt. 14:25-27).
- Calmed a storm (Matt. 8:22-27; Mark 4:39).
- Rose from the dead (Luke 24:39; John 20:27).
- Appeared to His disciples after His resurrection (John 20:19).

Trustworthy eyewitnesses recorded the miracles of Jesus. Ancient sources outside the Bible, such as the Talmud (a central text of Rabbinic Judaism), also make reference to His miracles. It is a non-Christian writing that attributes His miracles to magic and sorcery, yet he would not have described 'magic' and 'sorcery' unless there were supernatural things Jesus was doing.[62]

> Our rabbis taught Jesus the Nazarene had five disciples, and these are they: *Matthai, Naqqai, Netzer, Buni, and Todah.*
>
> The master said: *Jesus the Nazarene practiced magic and deceived and led Israel astray.*

---

[62] http://en.wikipedia.org/wiki/Jesus_in_the_Talmud

> On (Sabbath eve and) the eve of Passover, Jesus the Nazarene was hanged and a herald went forth before him forty days heralding, *"Jesus the Nazarene is going forth to be stoned because he practiced sorcery and instigated and seduced Israel to idolatry. Whoever knows anything in defense may come and state it."* But since they did not find anything in his defense they hanged him on (Sabbath eve and) the eve of Passover.

God used both fulfilled prophecy and abundant miracles to backup Jesus' claim of who He said he was. Christ's resurrection is an important miracle for which we will now discuss evidence.

Proof of the resurrection

The most important of Jesus' miracles was that of His resurrection. By it, He conquered death and sin. Even the Bible says that without it, our faith is useless (1 Corinthians 15:14). What proof do we have that it really happened?

Not only do we have the eye witness testimonies of the Bible, the events are also recorded by first and second century non-Christian historians, including Josephus, Tacitus, Thallus, and Phelgon.

As you will read below, the biblical accounts mention an eclipse and earthquake associated with Jesus' death and resurrection – the non-biblical accounts also record these events, providing even more support that Jesus was God.

Biblical account of Jesus' death:

> It was now about the sixth hour, and there was darkness over the whole land until the ninth hour, while the sun's light failed. And the curtain of the temple was torn in two. Then Jesus, calling out with a loud voice, said, "Father, into your hands I commit my spirit!" And having said this he breathed his last. Now when the centurion saw what had taken place, he praised

God, saying, "Certainly this man was innocent!" And all the crowds that had assembled for this spectacle, when they saw what had taken place, returned home beating their breasts. And all his acquaintances and the women who had followed him from Galilee stood at a distance watching these things (Luke 23:44-49).

Biblical account of Jesus' resurrection:

> Now after the Sabbath, toward the dawn of the first day of the week, Mary Magdalene and the other Mary went to see the tomb. And behold, there was a great earthquake, for an angel of the Lord descended from Heaven and came and rolled back the stone and sat on it. His appearance was like lightning, and his clothing white as snow. And for fear of him the guards trembled and became like dead men. But the angel said to the women, "Do not be afraid, for I know that you seek Jesus who was crucified. He is not here, for he has risen, as he said. Come, see the place where he lay. Then go quickly and tell his disciples that he has risen from the dead, and behold, he is going before you to Galilee; there you will see him. See, I have told you." So they departed quickly from the tomb with fear and great joy, and ran to tell his disciples. And behold, Jesus met them and said, "Greetings!" And they came up and took hold of his feet and worshiped him. Then Jesus said to them, "Do not be afraid; go and tell my brothers to go to Galilee, and there they will see me." (Matthew 28:1-20)

Non-biblical accounts:

> "About this time there lived Jesus, a wise man, if indeed one ought to call him a man. For he was one who performed surprising deeds and was a teacher of such people as accept the truth gladly. He won over many Jews and many of the Greeks. He was the Messiah. And when, upon the accusation of the principal men among us, Pilate had condemned him to a cross,

those who had first come to love him did not cease. He appeared to them spending a third day restored to life, for the prophets of God had foretold these things and a thousand other marvels about him. And the tribe of the Christians, so called after him, has still to this day not disappeared." (Flavius Josephus: Antiquities of the Jews, Book 18, Chapter 3, 3)[63]

"And with regard to the eclipse in the time of Tiberius Caesar, in whose reign Jesus appears to have been crucified, and the great earthquakes which then took place . . . " - Origen, "Against Celsus", Book 2.33[64]

"On the whole world there pressed a fearful darkness, and the rocks were rent by an earthquake, and many places in Judea and other districts were thrown down. Thallus calls this darkness an eclipse of the sun in the third book of histories, without reason it seems to me." (Africanus, in Syncellus)[65]

"Nero fastened the guilt and inflicted the most exquisite tortures on a class hated for their abominations, called Christians by the populace. Christus, from whom the name had its origin, suffered the extreme penalty during the reign of Tiberius at the hands of one of our procurators, Pontius Pilatus, and a most mischievous superstition, thus checked for the moment, again broke out not only in Judea, the first source of the evil, but even in Rome, where all things hideous and shameful from every part of the world find their centre and become popular. Accordingly, an arrest was first made of all who pleaded guilty; then, upon their information, an immense multitude was convicted, not so much of the crime of firing the city, as of hatred against mankind". Tacitus, Annals passage (15.44).[66]

---

63   http://en.wikipedia.org/wiki/Josephus_on_Jesus
64   http://www.neverthirsty.org/pp/historical-secular-quotes-about-jesus/phlegon.html
65   http://en.wikipedia.org/wiki/Thallus_(historian)
66   http://en.wikipedia.org/wiki/Tacitus_on_Christ

We can also look at how the actions of the disciples changed after the resurrection. Previously they were cowardly, deserting Jesus and running away when He was arrested (Mark 14:50). Seeing Him after the resurrection, they knew He was the Christ and became suddenly bold, proclaiming openly that Jesus was Christ and had risen from the dead (Acts 3:15, Acts 4:33). None of them recanted their testimony and endured torture and death as discussed in Part 4.

The Bible describes the over 500 witnesses who saw him alive on twelve occasions including:

- Mary Magdelene (John 20:10-18)
- Other women returning from the tomb (Matthew 28:9-10)
- Two disciples on the road to Emmaus (Luke 24:13-32)
- Peter in Jerusalem (Luke 24:34; 1 Corinthians 15:5)
- Disciples (except Thomas) and other followers (Luke 24:36-43; John 20:19-23).
- Disciples including Thomas (John 20:24-29)
- Seven disciples on the shore of the Sea of Galilee. (John 21:1-24)
- 500 believers at one time (1 Corinthians 15:6)
- James (1 Corinthians 15:7)
- Eleven disciples on a mountain in Galilee (Matthew 28:18-20)
- Disciples along the road to Bethany (Luke 24:50-53)
- Paul on the road to Damascus (Acts 9:3-6; 1 Corinthians 15:8).

These witnesses touched his physical body, saw the crucifixion scars and ate with him four times. His disciples testified that his resurrected body had flesh and bones (Luke 24:39), physical wounds (Luke 24:39), and could be touched and handled (John 20:27).

This is astonishing evidence that Jesus rose from the dead. No other religious leader such as Buddha, Muhammad or Krishna can make such a claim. Jesus however, was killed by trained executioners, buried in a guarded tomb then appeared to many witnesses having risen from the dead.

There is no doubt Jesus has impacted the world like no one else in human history. To me, the reason is clear – that He was who he said He was – God in the flesh – and was resurrected from the dead.

> "Jesus of Nazareth, without money and arms, conquered more millions than Alexander, Caesar, Mohammed, and Napoleon; without science and learning, He shed more light on things human and divine than all philosophers and scholars combined; without the eloquence of schools, He spoke such words of life as were never spoken before or since, and produced effects which lie beyond the reach of orator or poet; without writing a single line, He set more pens in motion, and furnished themes for more sermons, orations, discussions, learned volumes, works of art, and songs of praise than the whole army of great men of ancient and modern times." (Schaff, *The Person of Christ*, p. 29)

Despite copious evidence for the truth of the Bible and Jesus deity, opponents still raise objections which we will now explore.

CHAPTER 7

Objections to the Bible

Critics have raised various objections to the Bible and its teachings which we will now discuss.

You can't take the Bible literally

> Literal: "Taking words in their usual or most basic sense without metaphor or exaggeration" and "free from exaggeration or distortion", Oxford dictionary.

The Bible contains different styles of writing some parts are literal and some are figurative. We need to use common sense, experience and knowledge of how language works to interpret it correctly.

All works of literature including the Bible should be read as the author intended. In our everyday speech we use exaggeration, hyperbole and metaphors to communicate our message. For example, "I nearly died of embarrassment". Obviously, we don't mean we literally nearly died. Or a sports reporter might say one team "crushed" another – obviously they don't mean they are literally squashed on the ground. When Jesus is described as a 'lamb' it is not literally meant He is a lamb.

The Bible should be read with the same common sense approach. Many statements can be taken literally such as instructions to "Love your neighbour as yourself", "forgive others their trespasses" and "love the Lord with all your heart".

Different books of the Bible are intended to be interpreted differently. For example, the gospels of Matthew, Mark, Luke and John are eyewitness accounts and meant to be taken as historical records. Other Old Testament books are prophesies and others such as Psalm and

Song of Solomon are more like poetry.

The commands of Exodus were meant to be taken literally and obeyed by the people under Mosaic Law and although we can still learn from them today, we are not under the same law and do not have to take them 'literally' as the Jewish people were commanded to.

It is difficult to know how to interpret some books such as Genesis, as it is hard to know if the writer meant for it to be a literal historical account, or more metaphorical or allegorical. Interpretation of Genesis is still a cause of scholarly debate today.

Some parts are difficult for people to believe such as the creation account in Genesis, Jonah surviving 3 days in the belly of a fish, Jesus feeding 5000 with 5 loaves of bread or the Virgin Mary giving birth to Jesus. Therefore they don't want to take them literally even though the author may have intended a literal interpretation.

Similarly, people may not want to take literally parts of the Bible they don't like or disagree with. This might include issues around homosexuality or not wanting to believe God would send people to Hell.

With anything we read, we must ask ourselves – "what is the writer trying to communicate?" We can look at the genre (e.g. is it a letter, eye witness account, proverb, prophecy or historical account) and also at the whole passage of scripture rather than isolating a single verse.

Therefore, as with any literary work we need to discern those parts to take literally, but this doesn't discredit the truth of the Bible.

Isn't the Bible full of contradictions?

Some claim the Bible is full of inaccuracies and contradictions. Many alleged inaccuracies however, have been found to be correct once more archaeological or historical evidence has arisen. Most 'contradictions' within the Bible have also been resolved by Bible scholars. While some accounts may differ e.g. 1 angel vs 3 angels – this doesn't necessarily imply a contradiction. One person may have seen 1, one person many have seen 3 – both can be accurate accounts or testimonies. They would only be contradictions if one author said there were 'only one' or 'only three' angels there. Rather, this shows that the eye witness accounts are genuine. If someone had been fabricating the gospels, they would have ensured the accounts matched perfectly. That one of the accounts was not altered to match, shows the genuineness of the content.

Keep in mind, it may be our interpretation or knowledge that is lacking rather than an inaccuracy in the Bible, given we are prone to human error.

Has evolution disproved the Bible?

Surely the creation account in Genesis is not compatible with evolutionary theory? Whilst a literal interpretation of Genesis is not compatible with evolution, many biblical scholars have long seen Genesis 1 and 2 as an allegory rather than a factual account of history. Hence, a non-literal interpretation would render no discord with evolutionary theory.

Augustine of Hippo (4th century) and Philo of Alexandria (1st century) - long before the discoveries of modern science and evolutionary theory - are well known examples of those favouring an allegorical interpretation of Genesis over a factual or historical account[67].

The challenge with all biblical interpretation is to interpret it in a way that is consistent with how the author meant it to be understood by his audience. Whilst it is clear that books such as Psalms and Songs of Solomon should be read as poetry and that the Gospels are intended to be eyewitness accounts of actual events, it is not entirely clear how

---

67 http://en.wikipedia.org/wiki/Allegorical_interpretations_of_Genesis

Genesis should be interpreted. There is still much debate about this amongst Christians today and how this relates to science.

'Young Earth Creationists'[68], believe Genesis is a factual account of how life began just several thousand years ago and that all life forms were created in six literal 24 hour days with the human species beginning with a literal man and woman named Adam and Eve. At the other end of the spectrum are 'Evolutionary theists'[69] – those who believe God was the initial cause that started the evolutionary process, after which he did not have to intervene as natural processes took over. The middle includes the 'Intelligent Design'[70] movement who maintain that creation is the evidence of 'complex design' and 'irreducible complexity' and that God guided the evolutionary process. Others believe God performed multiple creative acts throughout the evolutionary process to create new species. They may accept micro evolution (small changes within a species) but reject macro evolution (evolution of one species into another).

There are a large number of Christians who support evolution whilst maintaining a strong faith in God. The Catholic Church, for example, officially supports evolution as being compatible with Christian beliefs. Many scientists, including Francis Collins, a well-known biologist who led the human genome project, sees no conflict between being a Christian and accepting evolutionary theory – his book "The Language of God" is good reading on this topic.

Supposing evolutionary theory is correct – would it have really served God's purposes to lecture ancient people on advanced evolutionary biology? A simple creation account that teaches timeless truths about God, sin and humanity that could be easily understood by both ancient and modern people would seem far more useful.

The Bible itself does not purport to be an in-depth scientific treatise -

68 http://en.wikipedia.org/wiki/Young_Earth_creationism
69 http://en.wikipedia.org/wiki/Theistic_evolution
70 http://en.wikipedia.org/wiki/Intelligent_design

what would scientists do?

> All Scripture is breathed out by God and profitable for teaching, for reproof, for correction, and for training in righteousness, that the man of God may be complete, equipped for every good work (2 Timothy 3:16-17).

Believing in evolution as a process does not mean that 'philosophical naturalism'[71] needs to be embraced- contrary to the assertions of atheists such as Richard Dawkins[72]. Philosophical naturalism, the belief that nothing exists outside the physical world, such as God or the supernatural, is often teamed with evolution by atheists to develop an all-encompassing theory to explain everything about life and humanity. As discussed earlier, 'evolutionary naturalism' fails to account for such phenomena as the moral law[73]. It also cannot explain how the process of evolution got started in the first place and the origins of the universe. As we concluded earlier, something can't arise from nothing.

With such a diverse range of views even amongst Christians regarding evolution and creation, you can surely be a Christian and have a strong faith in God without fully understanding the ins and outs of evolutionary theory or accepting it as true.

The crucial tenants of Christianity such as forgiveness of sins, reconciliation with God and Christ's death and resurrection should be the primary focus, as we cannot know for sure either way if macro evolutionary theory is correct.

---

71 http://en.wikipedia.org/wiki/Naturalism_(philosophy)
72 Dawkins, R. (2008). *The God Delusion.* Mariner Books.
73 http://en.wikipedia.org/wiki/Evolutionary_argument_against_naturalism

The Bible's teachings are outdated

Some reading the Bible may believe that some of the teachings related to slavery and the submission of women are outdated. It is important to place these in historical context though as for example, unlike the African slave trade which we are familiar with, in biblical times slaves were relatively free and were paid wages so could buy their own freedom if they wished. Similarly, women had practically no rights so the teachings of the Bible are actually very progressive in giving women more rights. If some of these teachings seem outdated to you, by all means, focus your attention on the central themes of Christianity such as Jesus deity and His death and resurrection which are teachings all Christians agree on and are not specific to a particular time or culture. Keep in mind though, our modern viewpoint is not necessarily flawless and may seem outdated by future generations.

Whilst legitimate concerns have been raised about the Bible and its teachings, I hope you will see these concerns are not valid reasons to discount the Bible, as it can be our interpretation that is at fault. Sceptics often will also have other doubts about Christianity, which we will now explore.

CHAPTER 8

Doubts & Objections to Christianity

Perhaps in light of the evidence you are open to the possibility that Christianity and the Bible are true. You might still have lingering questions or concerns though. This is perfectly normal. A few common objections and concerns which you may have, are discussed in this chapter.

How could a good God allow suffering?

There is no doubt there is much pain and suffering in our world – we see children starving, rape, murder and many other atrocities committed by humankind as well as natural disasters that destroy many lives. We may have experienced pain in our own lives for which there was no explanation. Many deny the existence of God or become bitter for this reason. They conclude that if God is all good and all powerful he wouldn't allow suffering and that its existence means that either God is not good – or he's not powerful enough or is too indifferent to stop it. Therefore, if He exists, He is certainly not worthy of being trusted or followed.

While it seems reasonable to us that a good God wouldn't allow suffering – we are overlooking the possibility that there could be a reason for allowing the suffering. This position assumes, 'if I can't see the point of the suffering, it must be pointless and wrong.' While I understand it can be hard to comprehend that there could be any good reason for the atrocities we see in the world – this doesn't mean there isn't a reason we cannot see. We can't assume our knowledge surpasses that of God's and that there is not some reason why an all-good, all-powerful God is allowing it to occur. Timothy Keller puts it well 'If our minds can't plumb the depths of the universe for good answers to suffering, well, then, there can't be any! This is blind faith of a high order.'[74]

We may have even seen this work out in our own lives in various ways. Perhaps something that seemed tragic at first, eventually led to something good that wouldn't have occurred otherwise. Losing a job at first may seem devastating but may lead to new opportunities if it hadn't been lost. We often hear stories of people who have suffered great tragedies or suffered illnesses and gone on to champion the cause and help thousands of others who are suffering.

The Bible is filled with stories of people who had to endure great suffering to bring about a greater good. Joseph's brothers sold him into slavery and he had years of suffering and imprisonment. Through these trials however his character was refined and he went onto save thousands of people from starvation. Jesus of course endured great suffering on the Cross which may have appeared pointless at the time – however it was to save humanity from eternal punishment and restore us to God!

Professor Peter Kreft as interviewed in Lee Strobel's "The Case for Faith" uses an excellent analogy of a bear caught in a trap by a hunter. The hunter wants to free the struggling bear but to do this, needs to shoot him full of tranquilisers. The bear however, thinks this is an attack and that the hunter is trying to kill him. To get the bear out of the trap, the hunter then has to push him further into the trap to release the tension on the spring. The bear would be convinced at this point the hunter was his enemy and out to cause him harm. However, he would be wrong as he does not have the understanding of a human being. Similarly, God's understanding and wisdom is far greater than ours and we have the choice to trust him or struggle. As Kreft puts it: "'How can a mere finite human be sure that infinite wisdom would not tolerate certain short-range evils in order for more long-range

---

[74] Keller, T. (2009). *The Reason for God.* (P.23) London: Hodder & Stoughton

goods that we couldn't foresee? Dentists, athletic trainers, teachers, parents—they all know that sometimes to be good is not to be kind."[75]

Even though we might not be able to see it now, surely it is plausible that there COULD be a good reason for allowing suffering that we can't see? One such explanation is endowing human beings with free choice. Allowing humans free choice unfortunately means that we are free to harm ourselves and others which can cause much pain and suffering. For God to continually intervene or control our actions, would limit our ability to freely choose. It is quite possible that God considers the trade-off of giving humans free-will, rather than creating them as automatons incapable of evil as a necessary one to make so that we ultimately have the free choice to know and love Him, love others and to do real good in this life.

In the same way the universe is governed by laws of nature and most natural disasters are a result of these laws at work. When sin entered the earth, creation also became subject to "bondage to corruption"[76] and is eagerly waiting for redemption.[77]

The Bible teaches that while there is no denying there is evil in the world, God does not approve of it nor does he cause it.

> For you are not a God who delights in wickedness; evil may not dwell with you (Psalm 5:4).

> Have I any pleasure in the death of the wicked, declares the Lord God, and not rather that he should turn from his way and live? (Ezekiel 18:23)

While some might say that the existence of evil, means God can't be good, it would also be very difficult to conclude that God was evil

---

75 Strobel, L. (2000). *The Case for Faith: A Journalist Investigates the Toughest Objections to Christianity.* Zondervan Publishing Company
76 Romans 8:21
77 Romans 8:19

based on the love, beauty and good in the world.

Evil provides evidence for God?

Strangely, rather than being evidence against God, the existence of evil and suffering can actually provide evidence FOR the existence of God.

By making judgements about what is good and evil in the world, we again come face to face with the moral law. Who determines what is right or wrong, good or evil, fair or unfair? We discover again we are moral creatures with an innate sense of right and wrong and desire for justice.

C.S. Lewis describes why he turned from atheism to a belief in God:

> "My argument against God was that the universe seemed so cruel and unjust. But how had I got this idea of just and unjust? A man does not call a line crooked unless he has some idea of a straight line. What was I comparing this universe with when I called it unjust?"... Of course I could have given up my idea of justice by saying it was nothing but a private idea of my own. But if I did that, then my argument against God collapsed too – for the argument depended on saying that the world was really unjust, not simply that it did not happen to please my private fancies... ". [78]

On what basis are we judging the world to be cruel and wrong? Again we are pointed to some kind of objective standard for right or wrong which can only come from a being higher than humanity such as God.

People understandably want to blame someone for their pain and they point to God, concluding if there is a God, He is not good. They don't realise that by doing so they are putting their own knowledge of good and evil above that of God's. If we deny the existence of God

[78] Lewis, C.S. (1960) *Mere Christianity.* Macmillon. P.31

BECAUSE of pain and suffering, we fall into the quandary of 'who's to say?' whether something is right or wrong, good or evil. If there's no objective standard such as God's, what we consider evil can only be a matter of personal preference.

Whilst this doesn't make the suffering easier, the truth can be eye opening when people realise what their judgement of good and evil means in terms of a Creator.

No matter what Christians endure as seemingly pointless suffering – they can be reassured that God is ultimately in control working things out for good.

> And we know that for those who love God all things work together for good, for those who are called according to his purpose (Romans 8:28).

The Bible teaches that there will indeed be suffering on this earth but that all things will be restored to us on the 'new earth' in a way that will make past pains and sufferings appear trivial.

> For I consider that the sufferings of this present time are not worth comparing with the glory that is to be revealed to us (Romans 8:18).

It also teaches that even during suffering we can rejoice and have hope.

> More than that, we rejoice in our sufferings, knowing that suffering produces endurance, and endurance produces character, and character produces hope, and hope does not put us to shame, because God's love has been poured into our hearts through the Holy Spirit who has been given to us (Romans 5:3-5).

Aren't miracles impossible?

Miracles are an important part of the Christian faith. Examples include

Mary's conception of Jesus, Jesus rising from the dead as well as all the miracles Jesus and his disciples performed such as healing people, feeding multitudes, raising the dead and turning water into wine. There are also a large number of miracles in the Old Testament such as Jonah surviving three days in the belly of a fish and the parting of the Red Sea.

Some people say miracles are not possible as they can't be scientifically verified and reject religion and the Bible because of its claims to miracles. However, just because they cannot be scientifically verified does not mean they are not possible.

By definition, a miracle is something that is attributed to God or to a divine agency.

Miracle (Oxford dictionary):

> An extraordinary and welcome event that is not explicable by natural or scientific laws and is therefore attributed to a divine agency[79]

The very nature of science means it is not equipped to verify miracles as it relies on observation and replication. Miracles however are one off occurrences and not subject to the physical realm – therefore science is not a valid way to assess the supernatural.

Some people may deny that a miracle actually happened (e.g. the resurrection of Jesus) based not on historical investigation but on the philosophical argument that miracles can't occur. No one can reasonably claim 'no miracles have ever occurred' because they cannot possibly have undertaken all the necessary investigation required to verify this for all the reported miracles throughout history.

If someone believes in God, miracles are entirely possible for an all-powerful God. If God created the universe, it is not hard to believe he

---

79   http://www.oxforddictionaries.com/definition/english/miracle

can rearrange parts of the natural world as He chooses.

For those who are dubious of miracles, the real problem likely lies in an acceptance of God. Miracles require supernatural intervention which is impossible with an atheistic mindset. Atheists have no frame of reference or way to explain miracles; however this doesn't mean they are not possible.

Why doesn't God do miracles more often to prove His existence?

Some people say they would believe in God if He would do a miracle or show Himself to them. Unfortunately, this was not what happened in the past when God did miracles. In the Old Testament, the Israelites saw many miracles, such as the parting of the Red Sea, yet constantly rejected and disobeyed God. Jesus also did numerous miracles, yet most people did not believe in Him. Perhaps they were amazed for a short time but then they would fall away. Jesus explained this in a parable, where a rich man finding himself in Hell, asks Abraham across the divide in Heaven, to send someone back from the dead to warn his brothers so they also wouldn't go there (Luke 16: 19-31). However, Abraham replies, 'If they do not hear Moses and the Prophets, neither will they be convinced if someone should rise from the dead' Luke 16:31. This is very prophetic of course, because even with the great miracle of Jesus rising from the dead (his body has still not been found), the majority of people still don't believe.

Whilst God does still do miracles (here is a website with some video testimonies)[80], we should not expect Him to do so like He did in Biblical times. God typically performed miracles in biblical times to present a new revelation or truth to His people to get their attention. This is why Jesus performed so many miracles – so people would really know He was the son of God.

---

80 http://www.cbn.com/700club/features/amazing/#healingmiracles

> "…even though you do not believe me, believe the works, that you may know and understand that the Father is in me and I am in the Father" (John 10:38).

Similarly, God confirmed the message about Jesus proclaimed by the apostles, such as Paul and Barnabas at Iconium, by accompanying their words with signs and wonders.

> .. Bore witness to the word of his grace, granting signs and wonders to be done by their hands (Acts 14:3).

So, God does not do important miracles just to entertain or amuse, but to communicate the truth of His Word when providing new revelation.

God also respects our free choice to either love Him or not. He could easily overwhelm us with miracles and force us to believe but as C.S. Lewis says "God cannot ravish, he can only woo". God makes it easy for us to ignore Him if we want to. At the same time, for those who want to know Him, He leaves enough clues so they can find Him.

In addition, if God performed miracles continuously they would lose their 'specialness' and when God really did want to communicate something important, they would have no impact.

So, whilst there are many reported cases of miracles today and I have witnessed some, don't expect God to perform miracles like a circus performer or to necessarily do large scale miracles like He did in biblical times. Although, people may think they will believe if they see a miracle, history has shown they will not.

How can a loving God send people to Hell?

God doesn't send anyone to Hell. He does all He can to keep us out of there. In particular, He sacrificed His own son Jesus to keep us out of Hell.

God is both perfectly loving and perfectly just. Every person has failed to live up to God's moral law so is guilty before Him.

> None is righteous, no, not one; no one understands; no one seeks for God.
>
> All have turned aside; together they have become worthless; no one does good, not even one (Romans 3:10-12).
>
> All have sinned and fall short of the glory of God (Romans 3:23).

God has given us free will, so we are free to choose whether or not to sin and to choose whether or not to love and follow Him. When we choose to sin, we are also choosing death and separation from God.

> The wages of sin is death (Romans 6:23).

Because we are all sinners and have rejected Him, by God's standards of perfect justice we all deserve to go to Hell, yet He does not wish for anyone to perish.

> Have I any pleasure in the death of the wicked, declares the Lord GOD, and not rather that he should turn from his way and live? (Ezekiel 18:23)
>
> The Lord is… not wishing that any should perish, but that all should reach repentance (2 Peter 3:9).
>
> God our saviour, who desires all people to be saved and to come to the knowledge of the truth (1 Timothy 2:3-4).

Because God doesn't want anyone to go to Hell, He sent Jesus to save us and take the punishment for our sin upon Himself on the cross.

> This is love: not that we loved God, but that he loved us and sent his Son as an atoning sacrifice for our sins (1 John 4:10, NIV).

Because God's perfect justice must be met, sins must be punished. If we reject the forgiveness and pardon for our sins offered by Jesus, there is no one else to pay the penalty for our sins except ourselves.

Some think that Hell is an overkill punishment for sin as our sins are finite yet Hell is infinite. This is overlooking the point that those in Hell don't suddenly accept God and start loving Him. They go on hating and rejecting Him. They have also transgressed an infinite being and therefore deserve infinite punishment. In addition, whilst our various sins might be finite, the sin of rejecting God himself is in a different category and is worthy of eternal damnation.

Why can't God create beings with free-will and have them all choose Himself? Although God is all powerful, he cannot do what is logically impossible. God cannot <u>make</u> someone <u>freely</u> choose Him. This would be a contradiction. Whilst God makes every effort to save people, some will exercise free will to not choose Him.

The question of "How can a loving God send people to Hell?", points again to the prevalence of the moral law as we are claiming that God is unjust in His judgements by sending people to Hell. Again, how did we come about these moral judgements and what is the objective standard for fairness? It is very shaky ground to presume our standards for justice are more objective or fair than God's.

What about those who have not heard of Jesus? The Bible says a knowledge of God and His moral law has been imparted to all people so all will be judged according to the knowledge they have been given.

> For his invisible attributes, namely, his eternal power and divine nature, have been clearly perceived, ever since the creation of the world, in the things that have been made. So they are without excuse (Romans 1:20-22, ESV).

> For when Gentiles, who do not have the law, by nature do what the law requires, they are a law to themselves, even though

they do not have the law. They show that the work of the law is written on their hearts, while their conscience also bears witness, and their conflicting thoughts accuse or even excuse them (Romans 2:14–15).

So in order to uphold His perfect standards of justice, people must be punished for their sin. God gives people every opportunity to repent but if they choose to reject Him, they must pay the penalty themselves.

Religion is divisive

When people think their religion is correct, they may be tempted to look down on or exclude those with alternatives beliefs and practises. Therefore it is true that religious beliefs have the potential to divide people but this is certainly not what Christianity teaches.

Christians believe all people are created in the image of God and they are therefore capable of good and are to be loved and respected.

The Bible stresses that no one should act superior to non-Christians as it is by grace alone they have been saved and therefore must not boast.

> For by grace you have been saved through faith. And this is not your own doing; it is the gift of God, not a result of works, so that no one may boast (Ephesians 2:8-9).

Again Paul says:

> "What becomes of our boasting? It is excluded. By what kind of law? By a law of works? No, but by the law of faith" (Romans 3:27).

Indeed, we are not even capable of accepting Christ, unless the Father draws us.

> No one can come to me unless the Father who sent me draws him. And I will raise him up on the last day (John 6:44).

Because Christians are not accepted by their good works but by faith in God alone, they acknowledge non-believers may be more morally upright or kinder than they are at times. Yet that is not why they are accepted by God. The worst sinners can come to God morally bankrupt and still be accepted by Him. As Abigail Van Buren describes, "a church is a hospital for sinners, not a museum for saints."

> "Those who are well have no need of a physician, but those who are sick. I came not to call the righteous, but sinners" (Mark 2:17).

Jesus says to the morally upright who think their good works will get them to Heaven "the tax collectors and the prostitutes go into the kingdom of God before you" (Matt 21.31).

The Bible teaches once we have accepted Christ, He begins the good work in us, to transform us into His image and adopt His good character (2 Corinthians 3:18) – but this is always a process – not a final destination. Christians may choose not to partake in some of the behaviours they used to engage in - but are always to be humble and to reach out to others in love and kindness.

> But when you give a feast, invite the poor, the crippled, the lame, the blind, and you will be blessed, because they cannot repay you. For you will be repaid at the resurrection of the just (Luke 14:13-14).

Because of this teaching, the early Christians mixed with other classes and races in a way that was shocking to those around them. Christianity does not require adopting Western or any other cultural practices and is compatible with all cultures. It has experienced explosive growth in Africa with 44% of the population now Christians and the same growth is now happening in Asia. This acceptance of other cultures was first demonstrated in Acts 15, whereby the Gentile Christians did not have to enter into traditional Jewish culture practised under the law in order to be Christians. Rather they were saved by grace alone.

Admittedly, not all Christians historically have practised the beliefs taught in the Bible of love, inclusiveness and tolerance – however these beliefs if universally accepted, would surely lead to greater peace in our world rather than divisiveness.

I don't like Church and/or Christians

For many people, their mistrust or dislike of Christianity comes from a bad experience with church or people who profess to be Christians but act in a way that is hypocritical, intolerant or not in line with Christ's teachings. The media also likes to create conflict and portray churches and Christians as backwards and/or intolerant.

I can understand this. I grew up going to a Catholic church and found the experience very disheartening. Each week, we would go to church, sit on hard cold benches and recite over and over the same liturgies and prayers. There was no sense of God there (for me anyway) and it seemed a lifeless, joyless place that my sister and I dreaded going to. I'm also sorry to say that in my 10+ years of attending, I never understood the Good News of the gospel – that Jesus died for my sins and that I was free. Free to love Him and have a relationship with God. It was not until I was older, that I encountered warm and loving Christians and a vibrant and joyful church environment that loved Jesus. Of course, Jesus is the one who spiritually 'awakened' me to His presence but the church I went to during childhood nearly put me off God and church for life! I had no idea that a warm and loving church environment existed where I could grow spiritually.

Others may have experienced hypocritical or condemning people who professed to be following Christ but were living or acting in a way contrary to the gospel teachings. The Pharisees in Jesus' day fit this description and Jesus didn't like them either. He frequently condemned them for pretending to be righteous and putting on a 'show' for others but inside having evil hearts.

In Mathew 23 Jesus lists all the hypocritical and prideful things they do and calls them 'blind guides' 'hypocrites', 'children of Hell', 'blind fools', 'serpents' and 'brood of vipers'. He condemns their many sins such as greed, injustice, pride, uncleanness and lawlessness and says instead they should have practised mercy, justice and faithfulness. The Pharisees were condemning others for the very things they were doing themselves and were meant to be teachers of the Old Testament law. Not everyone who calls themselves a Christian is truly following Christ.

In contrast, Jesus never condemned those who professed to be sinners and instead showed mercy to them. He frequently met and ate with sinners much to the dismay of the Pharisees.

> And as he reclined at a table in his house, many tax collectors and sinners were reclining with Jesus and his disciples, for there were many who followed him. And the scribes of the Pharisees, when they saw that he was eating with sinners and tax collectors, said to his disciples, "Why does he eat with tax collectors and sinners?" And when Jesus heard it, he said to them, "Those who are well have no need of a physician, but those who are sick. I came not to call the righteous, but sinners." (Mark 2:15-17)

I urge you not to be turned off Christ by previous bad experiences. Not all who profess to be Christians are really following the teachings of Christ. It is also important to remember as mentioned before that even genuine Christians are not perfect and to remember the analogy of churches being 'a hospital full of sinners' rather than a 'museum of Saints'.

Doesn't religion cause violence?

Many believe religion divides people resulting in war, violence and oppression. Whilst there certainly has been violence done in the name of religion which can't be excused, much more violence has been done by those who reject organised religion such as Communist Russia, Nazi Germany and the French Revolution.

Philip and Axelrod's "Encyclopaedia of Wars", which chronicles some 1,763 wars that have been fought during human history is enlightening in this respect. Of the wars chronicled, the authors categorise 123 as being religious in nature, which is a mere 6.98% of all wars. When wars waged in the name of Islam (66) are removed, the percentage is cut by more than half to 3.23%.[81]

Communist, Nazi and Marxist regimes have been a far greater source of lives lost as illustrated by deaths at the hands of various dictators below.[82]

>Joseph Stalin - 42,672,000
>
>Mao Zedong - 37,828,000
>
>Adolf Hitler - 20,946,000
>
>Chiang Kai-shek - 10,214,000
>
>Vladimir Lenin - 4,017,000
>
>Hideki Tojo - 3,990,000
>
>Pol Pot - 2,397,000

So while some wars have been waged in the name of religion, this is certainly not the norm despite widespread misconceptions.

Rather than wars being caused by religion, they are caused by sin as explained in the Bible. Sinful desires such as the desire for power, wealth, land or dominance over others lead to violence and destruction. Unfortunately, violent behaviour and wars occur regardless of the

---

[81] Reported by Robin Schumacher, http://carm.org/religion-cause-war
[82] Reported by Robin Schumacher, http://carm.org/religion-cause-war

beliefs a particular society has.

> "For from within, out of the heart of man, come evil thoughts, sexual immorality, theft, murder, adultery, coveting, wickedness, deceit, sensuality, envy, slander, pride, foolishness. All these evil things come from within, and they defile a person." (Mark 7:21–23)

Violence, evil, and war are opposed to Christian ethics. The Bible condemns murder, violence and oppression and exhorts Christians to love, patience and kindness and to care for the oppressed and marginalised. Christians are told not to retaliate but to 'turn the other cheek' (Matthew 5:38-40) and be 'peacemakers' (Matthew 5:9).

Whilst the evil that has been done in the name of religion cannot be excused, I would contend that much more good has been done in the name of Christ.

George Müller is an example of just one Christian who established 117 schools and cared for 10,024 orphans during his life.[83] You've likely seen many hospitals and schools with religious names in your own town. Thousands of charities and disaster relief agencies have been started in the name of Christ and uphold Christian values. In fact, their Christian faith is what caused them to make many sacrifices to help others. This is based on the realisation there is more than just this life and that Christ modelled and instructed a perfect example of reaching out to others. Mother Teresa is a well known example for her selfless work in helping others often in tough or dangerous conditions. Martin Luther King received the Nobel Peace Prize for combating racial inequality through nonviolence which was motivated by his Christian beliefs.[84]

Religious and humanitarian organisations are among the first to respond to a natural disaster or crisis. I am yet to see any Atheist

---
83 http://en.wikipedia.org/wiki/George_M%C3%BCller
84 http://en.wikipedia.org/wiki/Martin_Luther_King,_Jr.

organisations collecting for charity or providing aid/ disaster relief. So while it can't be denied that religion has caused harm, the good achieved by Christians cannot be overlooked either.

Christianity is an emotional crutch

You may have heard people proclaim "Christianity is an emotional crutch for the weak". However, if someone was merely after a 'comforting' religion, they could do a lot better than Christianity. Whilst the gospel certainly is good news, the Bible DOES NOT promise an easy ride once someone believes. Instead it promises "trials of various kinds" (James 1:2, 1 Peter 1:6). Jesus exhorts his followers to "count the cost" of following Him, saying "any one of you who does not renounce all that he has cannot be my disciple" (Luke 14: 25-35).

Many of the teachings of the Bible go against what we would naturally like to do or would be easiest. Christians are called to live in a new way of love and to no longer 'indulge the flesh' and sinful desires which can be difficult to do (Galatians 5:13). Many Christians experience anguish as expressed by Paul over the ongoing battle with sin (Romans 7:15). Other concerns for the Christian include knowing that unsaved friends and family as well as any deceased who did not accept Jesus are destined for Hell.

To me, this does not sound 'comforting' or easy at all. If someone was after an imaginary 'comforting' God, they could certainly do better than Christianity.

If Christians get comfort from the Bible or knowing God, it is because they have GOOD REASON to believe that God exists. Something is only comforting if you actually believe it. I could try to comfort myself with the thought that I can go ahead and run up a big credit card debt as money grows on trees so it will be no trouble to repay. However, because I don't actually believe this, I will get no 'comfort' from this thought. Unless you had good reason for believing God exists, you would get as much comfort from God as you would from the thought of money growing on trees.

The millions of Christians who are practising a faith in Jesus are doing so not because they want comfort but because they believe the gospel is true.

Is religion a product of evolution?

Atheists argue that everything about us can be explained as a result of evolutionary biology and a function of 'natural selection' including religious beliefs. Believing in God feels right to us not because God really exists but because this has helped us to survive.

They contend that religious feelings have evolved because they helped people survive in their environment and they passed on 'religious' genes to others. Evolutionists such as David Sloan Wilson theorise that the idea of a God brings people comfort, making them happier and more unselfish which meant their families survived and they got better mates. This of course does not explain religions and cults that DON'T promote unselfish behaviours and actually harm their members.

Other evolutionary naturalists (those who believe that nothing exists beyond the natural world e.g. spiritual or supernatural) assert that belief in God is an accidental by-product of traits that DID give competitive advantage.

There is a big problem with believing both Evolution and Naturalism are true as pointed out by Alan Plantinga.[85] If evolution without supernatural cause is true, then human cognitive faculties evolved to produce beliefs that have survival value, rather than to produce beliefs that are true. If human cognitive faculties are tuned for survival rather than truth, in accordance with assertions that belief in God is a survival mechanism - then why should we trust our cognitive faculties about

85 http://en.wikipedia.org/wiki/Evolutionary_argument_against_naturalism

anything at all – including what they are telling us about evolution and naturalism? On the other hand if we're created in the 'image of God', by way of evolution or any other means, then Plantinga argues our faculties would be reliable.

If atheists claim our cognitive faculties about God are wrong because they are a product of 'survival instincts', then they could be wrong about everything. It is self-defeating in that atheists can no longer rely on the 'laws of logic' to support their arguments. How we see the world is not necessarily correct – instead how we see the world is designed to give us an evolutionary advantage – whether this is a true representation or not. Charles Darwin also found this troubling:

> "the horrid doubt always arises whether the convictions of man's mind, which has been developed from the mind of lower animals, are of any value or at all trustworthy."[86]
>
> — Charles Darwin, to William Graham 3 July 1881

So, if we can't trust logic and our sense perceptions about God – we can't trust them about anything at all. Evolutionary naturalism also fails to account for the moral law, issue of human rights and universal desire for God as discussed in part two. Whilst evolution may be able to explain how life developed on earth, it does not tell us how this life and the universe got started in the first place! By trying to use evolution to account for everything about us rather than simply how life evolved on earth – it has entered the realm of philosophy rather than science.

---

[86] "Darwin Correspondence Project — Letter 13230 — Darwin, C. R. to Graham, William, 3 July 1881". Retrieved 2009-05-15.

Becoming a Christian will restrict my freedom

Some believe that becoming a Christian is too restrictive. They want to be free to live life on their terms, when and how they want without being accountable to anyone, especially God.

Whilst we get far more from knowing God than we could ever hope or imagine, there are certainly costs to following Jesus. We are no longer our own Lord and Master but become 'bondservants of Christ'. We are called to love the Lord with all our heart, body, mind and strength, because He is worthy of nothing less (Luke 10:27).

All relationships require give and take and adjusting our desires to that of the other person. Any one way relationship would turn into a dictatorship and would result in a loss of trust and intimacy. Surely with God it must be His way or the highway? Nope – God made the ultimate sacrifice in Jesus. He lost all dignity by being beaten, ridiculed and tortured on a Cross, just so He could be reconciled to us.

Likewise, we need to adjust some of our sinful habits and attitudes so we are more in line with God's desires. Avoiding certain behaviours and attitudes is not necessarily a restriction of freedom but rather a liberation from things that bind us.

> Jesus answered them, "Truly, truly, I say to you, everyone who commits sin is the slave of sin." (John 8:34)

> You have been set free from sin and have become slaves to righteousness (Romans 6:18, NIV).

In life, certain voluntary restrictions enable us greater freedom to pursue worthwhile activities. For example, a top sports person will give up certain activities and freedoms in order to become elite at their sport. We have to make choices every day as to what our priorities will be. Some choices will lead to good outcomes for us, some to poor outcomes. God has given us a 'guidebook' in the form of the Bible as to which thoughts, attitudes and actions are beneficial for us, pleasing to Him and will achieve His purpose for our lives. Feeling that God is restricting us from things, shows a misunderstanding of His character. He loves us!! Like any good father He is not giving us restrictions in order to cause us pain or frustration. He knows what is best for us and as we quickly (or slowly!) learn when we become Christians, it really is best to follow His guidelines. We will no doubt learn from our mistakes when we disobey His commands as there are likely to be negative consequences in our lives. This is not necessarily because God is punishing us, but is simply due to the law of cause and effect. We cheat on a spouse – this results in divorce. We are dishonest with taxes – we get fined. We are selfish towards others – they don't want to spend time with us.

Any love relationship or deep friendship will result in sacrifices but we willingly do this because we love the person. We will do things for the friend or lover that may restrict our freedom or independence like helping them when we would rather be doing something else. When we enter into a marriage, it is because we willingly want to be with only that person. It does not feel like we are making a sacrifice by committing ourselves to that one person.

Upon becoming a Christian, habitual sins will become abhorrent to us and we'll find ourselves not wanting to do anything that might hinder our fellowship with God.

When we seek God and experience His love, we earnestly desire to make sacrifices and serve Him. Going to church becomes a joy, not a chore. We desire to leave behind addictions and desires that are displeasing to God and embrace the new way of living. Sometimes to the chagrin of our non-Christian friends and family.

I'm not good enough to be a Christian

Some hold the false belief that we need to somehow 'clean ourselves up' before coming to God. This couldn't be further from the truth. Jesus specifically said he had come to call sinners, not the righteous.

> "Those who are well have no need of a physician, but those who are sick. I came not to call the righteous, but sinners." (Mark 2:17, ESV)

Time and again we see Jesus spending time with sinners and those who had been rejected by society, unlike the religious leaders and Pharisees of the day who shunned them.

This was my greatest concern about becoming a Christian. I didn't think I could measure up or be good enough for God. I felt certain I would let Him down and fail as a Christian. I was deeply aware of my own weaknesses.

Thankfully being accepted by Christ is not achieved by anything we do or through our good works but by grace alone. Otherwise, yes, I would have failed miserably at being a Christian! But I didn't understand the concept of grace at the time hence the reason for my doubts and fears.

If this is your concern as well, know that Jesus will accept you just as you are – warts and all – no matter what you have done… Really!!

Some of God's most prized men were the worst of sinners. Paul, one of the chief apostles used to persecute Christians before His conversion. King David committed adultery with Bathsheba during a time of weakness, then had her husband killed – despite having a harem of hundreds of women! Yet David was described as, 'a man after God's own heart' (Acts 13:22). Not because of His righteous deeds but because of his steadfast faith and enduring love for God.

Conclusion

Given the impact of adopting any belief system on your life, it is certainly prudent to address any concerns before making a commitment. If you still have lingering concerns that haven't been addressed, I urge you to continue your own investigation. Others have likely had similar concerns and information is freely available online and by talking to Christians.

If you are ready to move forward in your journey, part 3 takes a deeper look at what Christianity is and what accepting or rejecting Christ means for you.

PART 3

WHAT NOW?

CHAPTER 9

Accepting or Rejecting God

From the evidence we have discussed so far, you may be more open to accepting the truth claims of Christianity. But what does this mean and why do you need Jesus as your Lord and Saviour? How do you even become a Christian? Let's explore these questions now.

Who is the Christian God?

We learnt a lot about God in our study of the universe and humanity. The Bible confirms what we learnt and reveals more of His character. See: http://carm.org/questions/about-doctrine/who-god.

Importantly, God is eternal, has always existed and there is only one true God. God's nature is love. He is perfectly loving, just, holy, righteous, and merciful. God's holiness means He can have nothing to do with sin.

> Your eyes are too pure to look on evil (Habakkuk 1:13, NIV).

The Bible teaches that God is a trinity – comprising of Father, Son & Holy Spirit. There is only a single God but within Him are three persons. This is somewhat similar to a triangle in that a triangle has three distinct and equal sides but it is only one triangle. The three distinct persons of the Godhead can each love and communicate with each other.

> Go therefore and make disciples of all the nations, baptizing them in the name of the Father and the Son and the Holy Spirit (Matthew 28:19, ESV).

> The grace of the Lord Jesus Christ, and the love of God, and

the fellowship of the Holy Spirit be with you all (2 Corinthians 13:14).

The Godhead is highly relational and lives in mutual self-giving love that seeks to glorify each other. We see that throughout eternity the Spirit glorifies Jesus (John 16:4), the Son glorifies the Father (John 17:4) and the Father glorifies the Son (John 17:5). The Son demonstrated the ultimate love for the Father in that He was willing to die because the Father willed it. This 'other glorification' is the opposite of self-centredness and selfishness that often characterises our behaviour. As such, God is infinitely happy as there is an 'other-orientation' at the heart of His being because He does not seek His own glory but the glory of others.[87]

The trinity is difficult to understand but it is essential to God's nature of love. If God was simply one person, He would be unable to love until He created other beings. This idea of God as loving and personal is in stark contrast to Eastern religions that see God as impersonal and only concerned with the soul, not the material world.

Why did God create us?

God did not create us because He needed us or because He was lonely. He was perfectly satisfied within the trinity.

> The God who made the world and everything in it … is not served by human hands, as if he needed anything (Acts 17:24-25).

Despite not 'needing' us, God decided to create us anyway, out of love – in fact He has always loved us and loved us before we were even created.

> I have loved you with an everlasting love (Jeremiah 31:3).

---

[87] Keller, T. (2009). *The Reason for God.* London: Hodder & Stoughton

It was God's will to create us, He was pleased to do so and we were created for Him. God is a creative being who loves to create good things. He is also a relational being so created beings He could relate to. In short, He created us out of love and for love - creation was a natural expression of His love and goodness.

> Worthy are you, our Lord and God, to receive glory and honor and power, for you created all things, and by your will they existed and were created (Revelation 4:11).

> For by Him all things were created, in Heaven and on Earth, visible and invisible, whether thrones or dominions or rulers or authorities—all things were created through Him and for Him (Colossians 1:16).

From the beginning of time, God's plan was love. Historian George Marsden summarises Jonathan Edward's idea:

> God created us to "extend that perfect internal communication of the triune God's goodness and love... The universe is an explosion of God's glory. Perfect goodness, beauty and love radiate from God and draw creatures to ever increasingly share in the Godhead's joy and delight... The ultimate end of creation, then is union in love between God and loving creatures". [88]

God created us as an extension of His glory considering we were created in the image of God (Genesis 1:27). There are billions of people - all reflecting God's glory - as well as the universe and creation!

As we are made in His image and likeness we can know, love, serve, worship and be in relationship with Him. It is quite amazing that a perfect and holy God would allow us to know Him and be His 'friends'.

---

[88] George Marsden, Jonathan Edwards: A Life (Yale University Press, 2003), pp 462-63, cited in Keller, T. (2009). *The Reason for God.* (P.218) London: Hodder & Stoughton

"When I look at your Heavens, the work of your fingers ... what is man that you are mindful of him, the son of man that you care for him?" (Psalm 8:3-4).

> No longer do I call you servants, for the servant does not know what his master is doing; but I have called you friends, for all that I have heard from my Father I have made known to you (John 15:15).

Heaven & Hell

The Bible teaches that accepting God results in entering Heaven and obtaining eternal life, whilst rejecting Him results in eternal judgement in Hell. We will review Heaven and Hell now.

What is Heaven like?

The Bible describes three Heavens – the first is the sky, the second is outer space, the third is God's dwelling place where the souls of Christians who have died are. It is described as having the "glory of God", and "radiance like a most rare jewel, like a jasper, clear as crystal" (Rev 21:11). There will certainly be no more pain, suffering or tears (Rev 21:4) and the best part will be the glorious presence of God.

The 'New Earth'

Unlike other religions, the Bible doesn't teach that the end of the world will result in the Earth melting away and souls departing to Heaven.

Instead it teaches that when Christ returns, the Earth and its creatures will be RESTORED to perfection. Heaven will descend upon the world and it will become the 'new Jerusalem' and will be a 'new Heaven and new Earth' where we will live. Nature will be restored to perfection and humanity will be restored to love, peace and unity.

Do good people go to Heaven?

Most people think they will go to Heaven because they feel they are a 'good person'. An ABC news poll shows 9 in 10 people believe in Heaven and of those, 85% believe they will go there. Only one in four people believe access to Heaven is limited to Christians.[89]

The concept of God determining who goes to Heaven by comparing our good deeds to our bad deeds sounds reasonable but it is not reflected in the Bible. Heaven is in fact reserved for those who have been made 'holy' by the redemptive sacrifice of Jesus on the cross, not those who are good (Titus 3:5). Whilst we might think we are good, by God's perfect and holy standards no one is good.

> They have all fallen away; together they have become corrupt; there is none who does good, not even one (Psalm 53:3).

> And as he was setting out on his journey, a man ran up and knelt before him and asked him, "Good Teacher, what must I do to inherit eternal life?" And Jesus said to him, "Why do you call me good? No one is good except God alone (Mark 10:17-18).

God sees and knows every thought and action and will judge all sins no matter how big or small. No one will be blameless before God. Because Heaven is reserved for the righteous, the Bible warns that in contrast to popular belief, most people WON'T go to Heaven.

> Enter by the narrow gate. For the gate is wide and the way is easy that leads to destruction, and those who enter by it are many. For the gate is narrow and the way is hard that leads to life, and those who find it are few (Matthew 7:13-14).

> Strive to enter through the narrow door. For many, I tell you, will seek to enter and will not be able (Luke 13:24).

---

89 http://abcnews.go.com/images/Politics/994a1Heaven.pdf

> On that day many will say to me, 'Lord, Lord, did we not prophesy in your name, and cast out demons in your name, and do many mighty works in your name?' And then will I declare to them, 'I never knew you; depart from me, you workers of lawlessness.'(Matthew 7:22-23)

> And a highway shall be there, and it shall be called the Way of Holiness; the unclean shall not pass over it (Isaiah 35:8).

The Bible also teaches that Heaven is also definitely limited to Christians. Therefore you must be forgiven by Jesus before being allowed into Heaven.

> "This Jesus is the stone that was rejected by you, the builders, which has become the cornerstone. And there is salvation in no one else, for there is no other name under Heaven given among men by which we must be saved." (Acts 4:11-12)

Is Hell real?

Just like Heaven, Hell is a real place. Jesus spoke of it often and it is described in terrifying terms! The Bible describes eternal fires, everlasting torment, fiery furnace and a weeping and gnashing of teeth. Those in Hell will be in agonising pain, with deep regret and mental anguish for not accepting Christ. There is an unbridgeable gap between Heaven and Hell with no way of escape. There will be no human contact.

> And the smoke of their torment goes up forever and ever, and they have no rest, day or night, these worshipers of the beast and its image, and whoever receives the mark of its name (Revelation 14:11).

> Then he will say to those on his left, 'Depart from me, you cursed, into the eternal fire prepared for the devil and his angels

(Matthew 25:41).

> And if your eye causes you to sin, tear it out. It is better for you to enter the kingdom of God with one eye than with two eyes to be thrown into Hell, where their worm does not die and the fire is not quenched (Mark 9:47-48).

> The Son of Man will send his angels, and they will gather out of his kingdom all causes of sin and all law-breakers, and throw them into the fiery furnace. In that place there will be weeping and gnashing of teeth (Matthew 13:41-42).

Who goes to Hell?

Because God is absolutely Holy, sinful creatures cannot enter His presence and must be separated from God in Hell. Those who have not accepted Jesus Christ, called the "faithless", will go to Hell away from the presence of God and pay the "wages of sin" (Romans 6:23).

> But as for the cowardly, the faithless, the detestable, as for murderers, the sexually immoral, sorcerers, idolaters, and all liars, their portion will be in the lake that burns with fire and sulphur, which is the second death (Revelation 21:8).

Is Satan real?

Satan is also real, although he is not a caricature with red suit and pitchfork like we see in the movies! God originally created Satan as 'Lucifer', which means 'light bearer' and he was the highest angel "the seal of perfection, full of wisdom and perfect in beauty". However, Lucifer became proud of his beauty and splendour and desired to make himself like God (Isaiah 14:13-14).

Satan is now the "accuser of the brethren" (Rev 12:12) and the "God of this world" who has "blinded the minds of the unbelieving so that they might not see the light of the gospel of the glory of Christ, who is the image of God" (2 Corinthians 4:4).

Although he can't take away a Christian's salvation, Satan tempts all people to sin and rebel against God.

> Be sober-minded; be watchful. Your adversary the devil prowls around like a roaring lion, seeking someone to devour (1 Peter 5:8).

Salvation, Sin & Jesus

Whilst Heaven sounds like a great place to go, Hell certainly doesn't. To secure an eternal place in Heaven you must accept forgiveness for your sin as offered by Jesus.

What is sin?

Sin is described in the Bible as a transgression against God's law (1 John 3:4) and rebellion against Him (Joshua 1:18).

God originally created us perfectly sinless but gave us free will to choose good or evil and to obey Him or not. God asked us to obey Him in not eating the fruit of the tree out of love and obedience but we failed to do so.

True love means obeying not only when it fits with our agenda and goals but out of love and a desire to please the other person. Jesus typified this in going to the cross. He was completely satisfied in loving relationship with the triune God, yet showed the ultimate selfless love towards both the Father and towards us by dying on the cross.

Everyone has sinned and broken God's moral law except Jesus, which made Him the perfect sinless sacrifice for our sin.

Are you a sinner?

God's law reflects His moral purity and holiness. God's 'moral law' instilled into all humans is a reflection of His character and to break His law is to greatly offend him.

If you have ever lied, stolen, cheated, lusted, coveted, been angry with someone unjustly or dishonoured your parents then you have broken God's perfect law and are a sinner. If you have broken any of the 10 Commandments, then you have fallen short of God's standard and will be judged and punished for your sins.

God's laws when broken are an offense against Him and because of His perfect justice, He must punish the sinner. We would not respect a judge here on earth if they did not convict murderers and other criminals. Similarly, God who is a perfectly just judge will punish people according to their sins. This punishment includes a separation from God because He cannot be in the presence of sin.

The Bible says all have sinned and fallen short of the glory of God (Romans 3:23) and our sins have separated us from Him (Isaiah 59:2) resulting in death (Romans 6:23) and wrath (Ephesians 2:3). Out of great love and mercy though, God sent His own son Jesus, to atone for our sins and be punished in our place so that we would not have to be judged.

Repentance

Whilst we certainly need to repent for the things we've done wrong and the ways we've transgressed God, we also need to repent from rejecting Him. Most people construct false gods instead of the true God and worship things which can be good things in themselves like sex, money, relationships, family and health. They put their trust in these things for fulfilment, security and identity rather than trusting in God. You may have trusted in your own moral goodness, kindness or even church attendance or involvement to win you over to God rather than trusting in Jesus Christ. However, none of these things will save us and we must confess and hand these things over to God.

> They exchanged the truth about God for a lie and worshiped and served the creature rather than the Creator, who is blessed forever! Amen (Romans 1:25).

You may have come to this realisation yourself. Perhaps you have tried sex, drugs, relationships, career success and the like and found them to be empty. We see this often with celebrities. They seem to have everything in terms of looks, fame, success and money, yet they are still not satisfied at the deepest level, can't hold together relationships and turn to drugs and alcohol to attempt to numb the pain and find meaning. Know that none of these things will satisfy you. Even if you were to gain everything in the world as many celebrities have, you would still have a deep longing and ache that only God can satisfy. As Jesus put it, "What good is it for someone to gain the whole world, yet forfeit their soul?" (Mark 8:36, NIV).

> Instead, in Jesus we find 'living water' (John 4:10).

> "Everyone who drinks of this water will be thirsty again, but whoever drinks of the water that I will give him will never be thirsty again. The water that I will give him will become in him a spring of water welling up to eternal life." (John 4: 13-14, ESV)

Jesus really is the only one who can satisfy the longing of your heart!!

Accepting Jesus for salvation

Before a person accepts Jesus, they are 'enemies' of God and need to be reconciled to him. Our sin separated us from a Holy God and broke our relationship with Him.

> For if while we were enemies we were reconciled to God by the death of his Son, much more, now that we are reconciled, shall we be saved by his life (Romans 5:10).

Because we have all sinned and fallen short of God's Holy standard, we need a Saviour who can put us in right standing and make us perfect before God. Only then can we come into His presence and become part of His family.

> For he who sanctifies and those who are sanctified all have one source. That is why he is not ashamed to call them brothers (Hebrews 2:11).

Part of accepting God is accepting Jesus as God. The Bible is clear that the only way to be saved is through faith in Jesus Christ alone (Ephesians 2:8-9).

There is no halfway. We cannot just accept Jesus as a 'good man', 'prophet' or 'teacher', He doesn't leave that open to us. If Jesus is not God as He claimed to be, then he's not good at all, in fact he's a lunatic for claiming to be God. However, if Jesus is who He says He is, our only response is to fall to the floor and worship Him as Lord.

This is the 'good news' of the gospel, that Jesus died for the sins of the world (1 John 2:2) on the cross, was buried and rose from the dead (1 Corinthians 15:1-4). This sacrifice turned away the wrath of God (1 John 2:2) and saved us from sin and death. He did this so we could be 'set right' and cleansed before God so we can know and love Him. By setting us free from the bondage of sin, we become a 'new creation' with the freedom to live right.

The Bible says Jesus is the only way to the Father God (John 14:6), has all authority on Heaven and earth (Matt. 28:18) and has the power to forgive sins Luke (5:20). We cannot 'earn' our salvation in any way.

Once we realise the only way to be saved is through Jesus, we must then put our faith and trust in Him and His saving work on the Cross. You don't have to wait for all your doubts and fears to go before accepting Christ. It is not your understanding that will save you but Him alone.

Timothy Keller explains this well:

> "The faith that changes the life and connects to God is best conveyed by the word 'trust'. Imagine you are on a high cliff and you lose your footing and begin to fall. Just beside you as you fall is a branch sticking out of the very edge of the cliff. It is your only hope and it is more than strong enough to support your weight. How can it save you? If your mind is filled with intellectual certainty that the branch can support you, but you don't actually reach out and grab it, you are lost. If your mind is instead filled with doubts and uncertainty that the branch can hold you, but you reach out and grab it anyway, you will be saved. Why? It is not the strength of your faith but the object of your faith that actually saves you. Strong faith in a weak branch is fatally inferior to weak faith in a strong branch."[90]

If you are not a Christian, accept Jesus as your Lord and Saviour so you can be delivered from the righteous judgement of God for your sins. Turn from your life of sin and believe and trust in Jesus and He will cleanse you of all sin. Rely on Him to save you and you will be given eternal life as He promised:

> For God so loved the world, that he gave his only Son, that whoever believes in him should not perish but have eternal life (John 3:16).

> If you confess with your mouth that Jesus is Lord and believe in your heart that God raised him from the dead, you will be saved (Romans 10:9).

---

90 Keller, T. (2009). *The Reason for God.* (P.234) London: Hodder & Stoughton

Accepting or Rejecting God

For the wages of sin is death, but the free gift of God is eternal life in Christ Jesus our Lord (Romans 6:23).

The sinner's prayer

We come into relationship with God and are saved by the blood of Jesus. To be saved you need to:

1. Admit you are a sinner and need a Saviour (Romans 6:23)
2. Realise you cannot be saved by your own 'goodness' or self-effort (Acts 16:31)
3. Accept Christ's payment for your sins as provided by Father God (John 3:16)
4. Acknowledge and follow Jesus Christ as your personal Lord and Saviour (Acts 4:12)

Here is a short prayer you can pray. It doesn't have to be exact but mean it sincerely from your heart.

> Dear Heavenly Father,
>
> I know I have broken your laws and my sins have separated me from you and I need forgiveness. I am truly sorry and want to turn away from my sin towards you. I believe Jesus, your son, died for my sins and was resurrected from the dead and is alive with you.
>
> Your Word says that if we confess Jesus as Lord and believe in our hearts that God raised Jesus from the dead, we shall be saved (Romans 10:9).
>
> I confess and believe this now and invite Jesus to be Lord of my life and to rule and reign in my heart from this day forward.

Please send your Holy Spirit to help me love, obey and honour you.

Thank you Jesus for dying for me and giving me eternal life.

Amen.

Know you are saved

The moment you accepted Christ, He came into your heart and now His Spirit and nature lives in you. You did not become merely a 'better person' but you've been 'born again' spiritually and are now an entirely new creation created in Christ's likeness.

> Therefore, if anyone is in Christ, he is a new creation. The old has passed away; behold, the new has come (2 Corinthians 5:17).

Don't rely on your feelings to let you know whether you are saved or not as we feel closer to God at some times than others. We walk by faith and not by sight (2 Corinthians 5:7). God has promised to never leave us or forsake us (Hebrews 13:5) so you can be sure He is always with you no matter how you feel. Satan may try to place doubts in your mind that "you're not really saved" or "nothing happened" but if you placed your faith in Jesus you are saved no matter how you feel as His word promises salvation for all who confess and believe that Jesus is Lord (Romans 10:9). Believe also, there is rejoicing in Heaven!

> Just so, I tell you, there will be more joy in Heaven over one sinner who repents than over ninety-nine righteous persons who need no repentance (Luke 15:7).

Always remember that it is your relationship with Jesus that saves you, not any good deeds we do in His name. We are saved through faith alone and salvation is a free gift from God.

God has forgiven and forgotten all of your sins so you don't need to feel guilty for them. From now on, turn from any sin in your life and seek His righteousness (1 John 1:9).

Like me, you may have attended a church previously but perhaps you now understand it for the first time. Regarding salvation, it doesn't matter whether you're returning to your faith or discovering it for the first time, God is equally pleased.

Doubts about Christianity

You may still be harbouring doubts, fears or objections about Christianity or its message. It can take time to grasp the concepts of sin, salvation, the resurrection. Identify what these are and seek to gain greater understanding both from books and from other Christians. Perhaps you are worried about what becoming a Christian will mean in terms of how your life or relationships will be impacted.

The thought of Christianity may make you nervous as I initially was. As I shared earlier, when I first made the decision for Christ, I was apprehensive that I wasn't up for the task. I started off very uncertain in my faith but the more I learnt about Jesus and got to know Him, the stronger it has become. Like anything new you learn, it will feel unnatural and strange at first. It took me a lot of learning and stumbling before I came to fully know Jesus as Lord and to leave a lot of the sin in my life behind. BUT, it is by far the best decision I have ever made and everything is possible, bearable and much more enjoyable with Jesus by my side

Given the huge impact this decision can have on your life and eternity, it is essential to keep seeking the truth. Start the process of learning and discovery now by spending time in a Christian church and getting to know its members. Most Christians will be delighted to help you work through any questions you might have.

Know that Satan will do anything to talk you out of Christianity so beware of any lies or obstacles He may throw at you. Instead, keep pursuing God and seeking the truth. He promises to give the truth to those who diligently seek it (Matt 7:7-11).

> Ask, and it will be given to you; seek, and you will find; knock, and it will be opened to you (Matthew 7:7).

Although you must do everything you can to find God, ultimately He is the Good Shepherd (John 10:11) and will find you. Ask Him to come and find you and to make Himself known to you.

Rejecting God

Some people will unfortunately choose to reject God even when presented with overwhelming evidence for His existence. Reasons may include:

1. Feeling like they don't need a saviour as they're basically a 'good' person. As we have seen however, this is not what the Bible teaches. To proceed with this incorrect thinking will result in judgement from God.

2. Others may be afraid of what it will mean socially if they are following Christ but their friends and family are not. In some countries, people may face persecution for their beliefs as did the apostles.

3. For others, they do not want to give up the things of this world such as wealth, power or sex to follow Jesus as illustrated by the rich young man who was not willing to give up earthly possessions to follow Jesus (Matthew 19:16–23).

4. It may also be a matter of the will in that we are resisting God's attempts to draw us near to Him.

"You stiff-necked people, uncircumcised in heart and ears, you always resist the Holy Spirit. As your fathers did, so do you (Acts 7:51).

If this relates to anything you are experiencing, I urge you to reconsider as it will have grave consequences for your eternal destiny.

A New Life

If you've accepted Jesus, you've made the wisest decision of your life. It is an amazing journey, with plenty of ups and downs. Here are a few keys to help you along your way…

Accepting Jesus as Lord, means your life will be radically changed. No longer do we live for sin and gratifying the flesh but we seek to know Him, obey Him, love Him and serve Him. As a new creation, we "put off the old self" which is corrupt and "put on the new self, created after the likeness of God in true righteousness and holiness". Ephesians 4:22-24 (ESV). This means a whole new way of living and thinking and God's Spirit inside you will empower you to change.

God is a God of love and this is also His greatest command to us as 'new creations'. He wants us to show this love to those around us and to glorify Him through 'good works' which is through obeying His commands and helping others.

> Love the Lord your God with all your heart and with all your soul and with all your might (Deuteronomy 6:5).
>
> Love your neighbour as yourself (Matthew 22:39).
>
> We are His workmanship, created in Christ Jesus for good works, which God prepared beforehand, that we should walk in them (Ephesians 2:10).

Whilst your goal is to turn from sin and live for God, know that you will still make mistakes as a Christian and sin - don't let this discourage you. Ask God for forgiveness and keep seeking after Him and walking in His ways. We're part of the war between God and Satan, in which we know God will gain the ultimate victory. Through faith in God, we can defeat Satan and his lies (Ephesians 6:10-18).

There is true joy and peace found in knowing Christ. No matter what happens, He is our rock. We have the promise of eternity with Him that will enable us to endure hardship in this life and work as 'good soldiers' for the cause of Christ.

Christian Community & Church

Becoming a Christian is both a personal commitment to God as well as living in community with other Christians through a local church. While our commitment starts as a personal one, we need other Christians to help us along the journey and to grow into Christ-likeness. When we are 'born again' as Christians, we become part of a new family – God's family of believers.

The best thing you can do upon becoming a Christian is to join a good bible-based church. The church is an essential part of God's plan for Christians and its importance cannot be underestimated. Here you will meet new Christian friends and learn how to have a relationship with God. You will need the support structure of a church to help you learn and grow as well as to serve and live out God's purpose for your life. You will be strengthened by worship and the preaching of God's word.

> And let us consider how to stir up one another to love and good works, not neglecting to meet together, as is the habit of some, but encouraging one another, and all the more as you see the Day drawing near (Hebrews 10:25).

Although you may have previously had a bad experience with church, there are so many excellent bible-based churches with loving people, please take the time to get connected to a community of believers. If you know any Christians, it would be a great idea to tell them about your decision, they will likely be delighted to help you find a church and follow Christ.

The Bible

Making God's Word, the Bible a central part of your life is also extremely important. You will learn all about God, yourself, His purpose and how He wants you to live. It is God's 'love letter' to you!

> Your word is a lamp to my feet and a light to my path (Psalm 119:105).

The sheer size of the Bible (66 books!) may seem daunting at first, as it is actually a collection of many different books. The best place to start is with the New Testament Gospels of John and Mark so you can learn about Jesus' work and ministry. After the Gospels, the book of Acts gives a history of the early church. Next is Romans, a letter written by the Apostle Paul to the early church. Be sure to also read Genesis which describes human origins, sin and how people live by faith.

As you read the Bible, think about what the passage means and how it is relevant to your life. There are many excellent Bible study plans to help you as well as devotional readings that explain what passages mean and invite you to reflect on what you have read.

Christian books will also be a big help on your journey and answer many questions you have.

Prayer

Prayer is how we communicate with God. You may feel awkward at first but God loves you and wants you to talk with Him. You can release all your concerns, frustrations and worries to God on a daily basis because you know He cares (1 Peter 5:7). Here is a simple guide to get you started with prayer:

- Thank God for what He has done for you and the blessings in your life

- Praise Him for who He is (He is worthy of our praise)

- Confess your sins and weaknesses and ask that He would help you with these

- Tell Him about any problems or challenges you are facing

- Ask for guidance as to how you should live

- Pray for others, that they may come to Christ

Many people find it helpful to have a 'prayer journal' and write down their goals and requests then document when God answers a prayer.

Promises of God

As well as the wonderful promises of salvation and eternal life for all who accept Him, Jesus has also given us many promises that will encourage you on your journey.

Nothing can separate us from God's love:

I am sure that neither death nor life, nor angels nor rulers, nor things present nor things to come, nor powers, nor height nor depth, nor anything else in all creation, will be able to separate us from the love of God in Christ Jesus our Lord (Romans 8:38-39).

God hears our prayers:

This is the confidence we have in approaching God: that if we ask anything according to His will, He hears us. And if we know that He hears us—whatever we ask—we know that we have what we asked of Him (1 John 5:14-15, NIV).

Accepting or Rejecting God

God will meet all our needs:

And my God will supply every need of yours according to his riches in glory in Christ Jesus (Philippians 4:19, ESV).

We can trust His Word:

"For truly, I say to you, until Heaven and earth pass away, not an iota, not a dot, will pass from the Law until all is accomplished" (Matthew 5:18).

He provides satisfaction for our souls:

"I am the bread of life; whoever comes to me shall not hunger, and whoever believes in me shall never thirst" (John 6:35).

He gives us truth and direction in life:

"I am the light of the world. Whoever follows me will not walk in darkness, but will have the light of life" (John 8:12).

He strengthens us:

I can do all things through him who strengthens me. (Philippians 4:13)

He gives us a full life (true abundance, not just wealth!):

I came that they may have life and have it abundantly (John 10:10).

Delight yourself in the Lord, and he will give you the desires of your heart (Psalm 37:4).

God has plans for our good:

"For I know the plans I have for you," declares the LORD, "plans to prosper you and not to harm you, plans to give you hope and a future (Jeremiah 29:11, NIV).

Rest for our souls:

Come to me, all who labor and are heavy laden, and I will give you rest. Take my yoke upon you, and learn from me, for I am gentle and lowly in heart, and you will find rest for your souls (Matthew 11:28-29, ESV).

Supernatural strength:

He gives power to the faint,
and to him who has no might he increases strength.
Even youths shall faint and be weary,
and young men shall fall exhausted;
but they who wait for the Lord shall renew their strength;
they shall mount up with wings like eagles;
they shall run and not be weary;
they shall walk and not faint. (Isaiah 40:29-31)

Victory in Christ:

We are more than conquerors through him who loved us (Romans 8:37).

Peace of God:

Peace I leave with you; my peace I give to you. Not as the world gives do I give to you. Let not your hearts be troubled, neither let them be afraid (John 14:27).

God will work out negative circumstances for our ultimate good:

And we know that for those who love God all things work together for good, for those who are called according to his purpose (Romans 8:28).

Deliverance from pain or affliction:

and call upon me in the day of trouble; I will deliver you, and you shall glorify me (Psalm 50:15).

With God we can overcome fear:

The Lord is my light and my salvation;
whom shall I fear?
The Lord is the stronghold of my life;
of whom shall I be afraid? (Psalm 27:1)

He will be with us through every hurt, struggle and temptation:

Even though I walk through the valley of the shadow of death,
I will fear no evil,
for you are with me;
your rod and your staff,
they comfort me (Psalm 23:4).

I am just scratching the surface here, God has made hundreds of wonderful promises to us, do read His Word to find these treasures.

Tell others

Christ is good news! There is a lost world that needs to hear about the beauty of Christ and what He has done for us. God has called us to a 'ministry of reconciliation' (2 Corinthians 5:18-19), which is to point people who are unsaved to eternal life through Christ Jesus.

Know that it is God who ultimately changes a person's heart and makes them receptive to the gospel so always pray that God would work in the hearts of the people you know.

Discovering your purpose

One of the best things about becoming a Christian is that you actually have a purpose. No longer is your existence a meaningless merry-go-round of events and activities until you die, you have God. You can know you were created especially by God for His good pleasure (Revelation 4:11) and that you're not an accident or product of chance that has evolved from a random germ cell millions of years ago.

> 'In him we live and move and have our being'; as even some of your own poets have said, 'For we are indeed his offspring.'(Acts 17:28)
>
> For you formed my inward parts; you knitted me together in my mother's womb (Psalm 139:13).

In contrast, all atheists can aspire to as described by well-known atheist Richard Dawkins is a world of "no design, no purpose, no evil and no good, nothing but blind, pitiless indifference".[91]

Living with a purpose will give you focus, motivation and passion as well as preparing you for eternity. You don't have to look for your ultimate purpose in relationships, career, hobbies, family or success. While these are good and worthwhile gifts from God, they can let you down as nothing in this life is guaranteed. God has designed us for eternity, meaning this life is just a temporary assignment and while we should make the most of every day to serve God, there is no sense getting too attached to this world. Whilst we are free to choose our career, hobbies and spouse, God has a much larger purpose for mankind which we all fit into.

This includes bringing God glory through loving Him and others, reflecting His character, serving others with our gifts and telling others the good news about Him. God calls us to glorify Him, not to feed His ego but because he wants our joy. We will be miserable if we focus

---

91 Dawkins, R. (1995), River out of Eden. pp. 131–32

our lives on ourselves, seeking to gratify our own desires and living selfishly. God is the only being we can reasonably pour out our love on that will more than reciprocate and will never let us down. Loving Him is 'risk-free' as we know He will never leave us or forsake us (Deuteronomy 31:6) so we don't have to hold anything back.

Christianity is not just about having our sins forgiven so we can go to Heaven. Instead God's plan is to restore and renew creation as we discussed earlier. Rather than trying to escape this earth, we are to take part in the work of renewing it.

Rather than relying on 'self-discovery' to find our identity and purpose, we discover it through a relationship with God. Rick Warren's excellent book "The Purpose Driven Life" explains God's purposes for us as Christians and how we can use our gifts and talents to love God and serve others.

5 Purposes – "The Purpose Driven Life" Rick Warren

1. Worship: We were planned for God's pleasure

Worship is about living to please God. He is pleased when we love, trust, obey, praise and seek to serve Him with our gifts and abilities. God wants our friendship most of all which we can develop through constant conversation (prayer), meditating on His Word, honesty and obedience. A true friendship with God means putting His interests ahead of our own as well as continuing to worship Him when He seems distant or we don't understand what is happening in our lives.

2. Fellowship: We were formed for God's family

Fellowship with other Christians will give us a place to belong and teach us how to love imperfect, frustrating people. You will be able to share life together and support and build each other up. We need to invest time and effort into cultivating community and friendships and seek to love each other unselfishly.

3. Discipleship: We were created to become like Christ

We do this by allowing God to mould us and by changing the way we think and act so it is in accordance with His Word. God will use His Word, our circumstances and even trouble and temptation to conform us into Christ's likeness.

4. Ministry: We were shaped for serving God

God has given us all different spiritual gifts, abilities, personality, interests and experience which he wants us to use for serving the body of Christ.

5. Evangelism: We were made for mission

Sharing the good news of God's grace to unbelievers is one of our primary purposes.

I would strongly recommend you get this book, it is one of the most helpful books I read as a new Christian.

Growing in Christ

Most people originally go to God because they want something. Often they are in a great deal of physical or emotional pain or are feeling lost, lonely or hurt. Whilst this is understandable, at some point we must come to the realisation that God is not here to serve us. We owe Him our lives simply for creating us and eternal gratitude for our salvation.

Once saved, it is important to stop doing those things that are displeasing to God. He will live in you and help you to change and resist sin. Although as a Christian you will never be perfect, God wants us to 'aim' towards perfection. We do this by submitting to His Spirit rather than our natural, sinful desires by following the example of Jesus and living a Godly life. When we grow closer to Jesus, this will lead us away from our sinful thoughts and behaviour. God wants us to walk in a way pleasing to Him and to increase in knowledge of

Him (Colossians 1:10). A sinful lifestyle and habits will lead us away from God and back into old ways which lead to death. Instead we should turn from these out of our love for God (2 Corinthians 7:1).

All of this will be achieved as we grow in our relationship with Jesus through studying His Word (the Bible), being part of His Body (the Church), in fellowship with Him (in prayer) and in relationship with other Christians.

The fruit of real faith is love – treating all others the same way you want to be treated.

> A sacrifice to be real must cost, must hurt, must empty ourselves. The fruit of silence is prayer, the fruit of prayer is faith, the fruit of faith is love, the fruit of love is service, the fruit of service is peace. - Mother Theresa.

Trials & suffering

Trials and suffering unfortunately don't end when we become Christians – as Christ underwent suffering, we also will.

> Beloved, do not be surprised at the fiery trial when it comes upon you to test you, as though something strange were happening to you. But rejoice insofar as you share Christ's sufferings, that you may also rejoice and be glad when his glory is revealed (1 Peter 4:12-19).

Trials can come in many forms including our own sin, circumstances beyond our control, or other people. Some particular things you may struggle with as a Christian include:

- Being hurt by other believers. There are certainly no perfect Christians and all are prone to sin - do remember that not everyone who professes to know Christ really does, so don't let it hurt your faith. At the same time, endeavour not to judge other believers until you have walked in their shoes.

- God may not meet all of your expectations and may even appear not to fulfil His promises.

- You may experience 'dry spells' where you can't sense God's presence. This is a great opportunity to live by faith in His word and not to rely on your feelings.

- You may struggle with certain sins for long periods, however resist condemnation (Romans 8:1)

It can be hard to go through trials and suffering at the time, however we can be reassured that even through suffering God "works all things together for good" (Romans 8:28). We discussed earlier that even though we may not be able to SEE any good reason for suffering or pain, this doesn't mean there isn't one. The most important thing to cling to is that God is real and that He loves you. He DOES have a good plan for your life even if it feels like things are caving in. Knowing this we can endeavour to "rejoice" in trials as they are helping to perfect our faith.

> Count it all joy, my brothers, when you meet trials of various kinds, for you know that the testing of your faith produces steadfastness. And let steadfastness have its full effect, that you may be perfect and complete, lacking in nothing (James 1:2-4).

When we become a Christian, we become 'mini Christs' and God desires us to become more like Jesus through a process of 'sanctification' in which we are 'refined' like gold.

> In this you rejoice, though now for a little while, if necessary, you have been grieved by various trials, so that the tested genuineness of your faith—more precious than gold that perishes though it is tested by fire—may be found to result in

praise and glory and honor at the revelation of Jesus Christ (1 Peter 1:6-7).

Trials can also help us draw nearer to God in that we realise nothing in this world is guaranteed to last such as wealth, health, relationships and success. Only when we let go of these things and are dependent on Him will we be truly free. God invites us to persevere with our faith through trials and sufferings and never to lose hope (Romans 5:3-5). He will surely reward us with the "crown of life" which He has promised to those who love Him (James 1:12).

We can be sure God will be with us through every trial (Psalm 23:4) and will not allow anything in our lives which we cannot bear (1 Corinthians 10:13).

Staying the distance

Your salvation is based on your 'continued' relationship with God and faith in Jesus. It is essential to keep living for and believing in Him and not to drift away. Believing in God and seeking after Him is an active process, not a passive one. It can be easy to let our cares and concerns in this world, choke out our desire for Him.

> but the cares of the world and the deceitfulness of riches and the desires for other things enter in and choke the word, and it proves unfruitful (Mark 4:19).

Know that the Christian journey is a 'walk of faith' with plenty of ups and downs. The worst thing that could happen is for you to give up on your faith when you get discouraged by life circumstances or sin or when it seems like God isn't there. During these times we need to cling to His Word and promises that He loves us and will always be with us. Reach out to mature believers in the faith who can help you through any difficulties as well as help you grow in Christ.

Remember that this Earth and life is not your final destination, you have a home awaiting you in Heaven and then on the 'new Earth' when God will restore all things. We have a great inheritance waiting for us with Him.

> He will wipe away every tear from their eyes, and death shall be no more, neither shall there be mourning, nor crying, nor pain anymore, for the former things have passed away (Revelation 21:4).

> But, as it is written, "What no eye has seen, nor ear heard, nor the heart of man imagined, what God has prepared for those who love Him" (1 Corinthians 2:9).

If I am not privileged to meet you in this lifetime, I definitely look forward to meeting you in the next life. At which point, as beautifully described by C.S. Lewis – we will be home at last!

> "I have come home at last! This is my real country! I belong here. This is the land I have been looking for all my life, though I never knew it till now... All their life in this world and all their adventures... had only been the cover and the title page: now at last they were beginning Chapter One of the Great Story which no one on earth has read: which goes on for ever: in which every chapter is better than the one before." [92]

---

92 Lewis, C.S.(2002). The Last Battle.HarperCollins; Reprint edition.

CHAPTER 10

Parting thoughts

Where else would we go?

If you are honest with the evidence, I'm sure you will agree 'beyond reasonable doubt' that God exists and Christianity is true. Science, humanity and the world we live in provides much evidence for God. No one other than Jesus has fulfilled prophecies, performed numerous miracles, raised the dead and risen from the dead himself: providing a way of salvation for mankind. Evidence for the Bible, New Testament and the person of Jesus compels us to conclude that Jesus is God as He claimed and Christianity is true. All other religious systems, including atheism can be found to be irrational, illogical or inconsistent with the scientific, historic and humanistic evidence. In addition, what they 'offer' fails miserably compared to Christ. For example, Islam will teach us to kill and atheism will leave us empty and purposeless. In the words of Peter, one of Jesus' disciples: "Lord, to whom shall we go? You have the words of eternal life, and we have believed, and have come to know, that you are the Holy One of God." (John 6:68)

Jesus is the only one who can provide us with the Truth we desperately need – indeed He is the truth.

> I am the way, and the truth, and the life. No one comes to the Father except through me. (John 14:6)

I pray that you have discovered greater Truth through this book and either deepened your Christian faith or started the journey towards God. Do continue your pursuit of Him, nothing compares..!

> You have multiplied, O LORD my God, your wondrous deeds

and your thoughts toward us; none can compare with you! I will proclaim and tell of them, yet they are more than can be told (Psalm 40:5).

Love & blessings,
Michelle

Acknowledgements

Editing & Proofreading

Huge thanks to Antonio Pavletich and Shawn Martin for their kind and generous proofreading of this text.

Resource Acknowledgements

Several important books have been referenced multiple times in the creation of this work and I sincerely thank the authors for their excellent work in this area. I highly recommend these books for further reading.

> Keller, T. (2009). *The Reason for God.* London: Hodder & Stoughton
>
> Lewis, C.S. (2001). *Mere Christianity.* HarperCollins Publishers
>
> Strobel, L. (2000). *The Case for Faith: A Journalist Investigates the Toughest Objections to Christianity.*
>
> Geisler, N. & Turek, F. (2004). *I Don't Have Enough Faith To Be An Atheist.*
>
> Francis S. Collins. (2006). *The Language of God: a Scientist Presents Evidence for Belief.* Simon and Schuster.

I have also drawn heavily on several apologetics websites due to their excellent information provided freely online. Thank you for your service in this area.

> http://www.gotquestions.org
>
> http://www.alwaysbeready.com
>
> http://carm.org

About the Author

Michelle is a born again Christian who loves Jesus and His Word.

A deep desire for people to come to know Christ and for believers to deepen in their faith and be confident sharing with non-Christians has inspired this book.

Having had her heart transformed by Christ, Michelle is now passionate about helping those in need and supporting charity.

Michelle believes developing great personal habits is a key to living effectively and serving Christ well. To overcome some of her own personal habits as well as help others, she wrote her first book "7 Steps to Make or Break Habits".

Michelle is a strong believer in health and fitness for mind, body and spirit to best serve the Lord. She enjoys fitness pursuits such running, cycling, gym and hiking.

Michelle is committed to life-long learning. Formal education includes a Bachelor of Arts in Psychology and a Bachelor of Commerce in Marketing & Commercial Law. Born in Wellington, New Zealand, Michelle moved to Melbourne, Australia in 2002 where she has since lived and worked

Printed in Great Britain
by Amazon